SONER CAGAPTAY

The Rise of
Turkey

THE TWENTY-FIRST CENTURY'S
FIRST MUSLIM POWER

POTOMAC BOOKS
An imprint of the University of Nebraska Press

∞

Library of Congress
Cataloging-in-Publication Data

Çağaptay, Soner.
The rise of Turkey: the twenty-first century's first
Muslim power / Soner Cagaptay.
pages cm
Includes bibliographical references and index.
ISBN 978-1-61234-650-2 (cloth: alk. paper)—ISBN
978-1-61234-651-9 (pdf: alk. paper) 1. Turkey—
Politics and government—21st century. 2. Turkey—
Foreign relations—21st century. 3. Turkey—Economic
conditions—21st century. 4. Islam and state—Turkey.
5. World politics—21st century. I. Title.
JQ1805.C338 2014
320.9561—dc23
2013034280

Set in Fanwood by Laura Wellington.

To my brother, Ali Cagaptay, for raising me, and my
friend M. Khairi Abaza, for teaching me how to write better

Contents

Illustrations

Acknowledgments

This book is a synthesis of my work over the past two decades, including my doctoral studies at Yale University and more recent scholarship at The Washington Institute for Near East Policy. I am grateful to both institutions for helping me find a place to write and for nurturing my ideas. I am also thankful to Rob Satloff, executive director of the Washington Institute, Patrick Clawson, its research director, and my colleagues at the Washington Institute, as well as the institute's donors for their support for my work over the past decade. More specifically I would like to thank Vanessa and Tony Beyer for their dedication to my work and the mission of the Turkish Research Program at the Washington Institute for Near East Policy. I am also grateful to Yvonne and Michael Silverman for their support for my work.

I am indebted to my research assistants and interns at the Washington Institute, a class of over forty people, who have helped me with my work over the past decade and have therefore contributed to this book. In this regard special thanks go to Hale Arifagaoglu, Katie Kiraly, Bilge Menekse, Altay Sedat Otun, Merve Tahiroglu, and Beril Unver for their help in improving the book. I am also grateful to my friends and colleagues at the Washington Institute and elsewhere who took the time to review various versions of this book, providing useful feedback and corrections. Additionally I extend my gratitude to the Washington Institute's executive editor Mary Horan for her skill in creating visuals for this book. Last but not least, I am indebted to my research assistant Tyler Evans and research intern Esin Efe, who have helped me tremendously with this book, doing research, editing, drafting paragraphs, and preparing visual material. Without Tyler and Esin, this book would not have been completed. Finally I owe gratitude to my friend Jen Moore for inspiring me to write this book. Of course, all the omissions and errors are mine.

Prologue

On November 1, 1922, the reign of the Ottoman Sultan in Istanbul officially came to an end. Shortly thereafter, bereft of the pomp and opulence of the imperial court, the once-mighty ruler of the Ottomans took a last lonely voyage to exile in southern Europe. The world had changed, and the Ottoman powers that had commanded a vast empire failed to keep pace. And so, broken by war and the changing tide of history, the sultan receded into geopolitical obscurity, stepping aside as a fledgling new Turkish nation-state grew out of the ruins. On this day in history precisely ninety years later, Turkey's new ruler, Recep Tayyip Erdogan, was on a trip of his own to Europe. But this voyage could not have been more different. Prime Minister Erdogan departed Turkey with great fanfare: the purpose of his trip was to open a gargantuan diplomatic compound in Berlin, Germany. The German *Frankfurter Allgemeine Zeitung* covered the leader's visit with the headline "Erdogan's EU [European Union] Ultimatum," a reference to Erdogan's impatience with the European Union for its reluctance to allow Turkey to join the club. Indeed, Erdogan's assertiveness was a reflection of Turkey's newfound confidence and its refusal to wait patiently at Europe's doorstep. In fact, Turkey is increasingly cultivating economic and political clout in its former Ottoman domains. And Erdogan's arrival in Germany brought into relief not only Turkey's vigorous outreach to the world but also the dramatic shifts in relative power and dynamism between Turkey and the West.

In today's world, terms that were once ascribed to the Ottomans, such as *sclerotic* and *brittle* are applied most often to the prostrate European Union. Whereas for Turkey (once the "sick man" of Europe) terms like *change* and *transformation* have become the watchwords. The dean of the School of Management at Yale University, my alma mater, sees Turkey entering the pantheon of top ten economies in the coming decade, adding, "Turkey is one of the pivot players in the world. I believe Turkey has reached the level of BRICS [Brazil, Russia, India, China, South Africa] countries long ago." In the months following the outbreak of the Arab Spring, U.S. president Barack Obama telephoned Prime Minister Erdogan more than any other world leader, with the exception of Britain's prime minister. In short, understanding Turkey is important for understanding the changing global order.

This book is a guide to Turkey's changes, both in their inspiring potential and in the grave obstacles they pose. The chapters ahead are a tour of the themes, challenges, and forces that are driving today's Turkey. Taking a journey from Washington to Istanbul, with stops across Turkey in between, this book takes a close look at the places and people that are reshaping Turkey and defining its role in the future of global politics.

Abbreviations

ANAP	Motherland Party
AKP	Justice and Development Party
BDP	Peace and Democracy Party
BRICS	Brazil, Russia, India, China, South Africa
CHP	Republican People's Party
CIS	Commonwealth of Independent States
DP	Democrat Party
DYP	True Path Party
EU	European Union
FTA	Free Trade Agreement
FDI	Foreign Direct Investment
GCC	Gulf Cooperation Council
GDP	Gross Domestic Product
IMF	International Monetary Fund
KCK	Union of Communities in Kurdistan
KRG	Kurdistan Regional Government of Iraq
MENA	Middle East and North Africa
MHP	Nationalist Action Party
NGO	Nongovernmental Organization
ODTU	Middle East Technical University
OECD	Organisation for Economic Co-operation and Development
OIC	Organization of Islamic Cooperation
PJAK	Party for a Free Life in Kurdistan, a PKK affiliate

PKK	Kurdistan Workers Party
PPP	Purchasing Power Parity
PS	Portuguese Socialist Party
PYD	Democratic Union Party, a PKK affiliate
RP	Welfare Party
SP	Felicity Party
SPD	Social Democratic Party of Germany
TEPAV	Economic Policy Research Foundation of Turkey
TESEV	Turkish Economic and Social Studies Foundation
TIKA	Turkish Cooperation and Coordination Agency
UEFA	Union of European Football Associations

Introduction | RISING TURKEY AND ITS CHALLENGES

In May 2013 millions of Turks poured into the streets of Istanbul in the dead of night. Marching on the heart of the city, the massive procession shouted slogans, banged pots and pans, and dared the authorities to silence their defiant act of free speech. The city convulsed with protests for weeks. The spark that ignited "the Gezi Movement" of June 2013 was public outrage at police treatment of a tiny group of environmentalists who were protesting the destruction of Istanbul's Gezi Park to make way for a shopping mall. Mainstream Istanbul may not have subscribed to the politics of these bohemian environmentalists, but they were prepared to passionately defend the rights of these individuals to free expression, even if it meant standing up to tear gas and water cannons. More than anything else, this points to the rise of Turkey as a middle-class society with democracy at its core.

This vibrant democratic flourishing is a profound blessing for Turkey, but its accompanying growing pains present a major challenge for the ruling Justice and Development Party (AKP). Over the past decade Turkey has become a regional economic powerhouse, largely thanks to sound policies implemented by the AKP. And as Turkey's citizens have benefited from this prosperity, they have awakened to the mindset of middle-class societies in the developed world. Respect for diversity and the sanctity of individual rights, the demand for a voice in democratic deliberation, and the many other trappings of contemporary democracy have all embedded themselves in the new currents of Turkish society.

1

Turkey has evolved dramatically over the past decade, and the ripples of this transformation are only just becoming apparent. Where does Turkey go from here? If countries could be vegetables, Turkey would be an onion. Every time you take off a layer of skin, hoping to get to the core, you come across yet another layer. Indeed, Turkey continues to astound me in its capacity to grow and transform. In 1970 I was born in Malatya, a mid-sized city in the Turkish heartland of Anatolia that took its name from the Hittites three thousand years ago. I then moved to Istanbul to attend a boarding school that overlooked the Golden Horn and sat only a stone's throw from some of the city's most prominent Roman, Byzantine, and Ottoman monuments. I always wanted to be a historian. Growing up in Turkey, this seemed only natural. By now I have spent nearly half my life studying and working in the United States. But as a historian and observer of Turkish politics, I return frequently to Turkey to get a snapshot of how things are changing.

I remember leaving Turkey for the first time as a high school student in the 1980s to study abroad at a high school in the forests of California. Before I left, I had to plead to get my hands on two hundred dollars to bring to the United States for expenses. Scouring the oppressively humid bureaucratic hallways in the Istanbul summer, I searched for a clerk who might show some sympathy and help me procure this paltry sum. I was facing these difficulties because there were strict restrictions on holding foreign currency in Turkey at the time. Finally, I did manage to put together the needed funds, and I spent my senior year of high school in rural California, far from the bustle of Istanbul. This was before the Internet age, and even long-distance calls were pushing the limits of Turkey's infrastructure at the time, so I had little ability to keep up with events in my country of birth, apart from the occasional scrap of news in local papers. After only a year away from home, imagine my surprise when I landed in Istanbul to see foreign products lining the store shelves, many with prices quoted in dollars! As I quickly discovered, in my absence Turkey had lifted its currency restrictions, and many Turks were rushing to the bank to open accounts in U.S. dollars and German marks.

This was only one of the many fundamental reforms to emerge during the 1980s from the forward-looking vision of Turkey's then prime minister Turgut Ozal, who made the decision to open the country's economy to the world. As I later realized, Ozal not only set the stage for Turkey's meteoric rise under the AKP over the past decade, but he also fastened Turkey to the economies of the Western world, with irreversible consequences for Turkey's political destiny.

Turkey managed to surprise me again two decades later when I took a trip to the southeastern city of Gaziantep. Having witnessed the blossoming of Turkey's Western metropolitan hubs—namely Istanbul, Ankara, and Izmir—I had come under the impression that globalization had split Turkey apart economically. On the one hand the Westernized elite had plugged into the global economy to become cosmopolitan and wealthy; meanwhile Turkey's Anatolian towns had been left in the dust, or so I thought.

Stepping onto the medieval city center, I was struck by just how wrong I was. The poverty and provincialism I remembered from previous visits was vanishing, and in its place was rising an Anatolian city I never could have expected while growing up in Turkey. I sat down in a café to overhear Turkish businessmen discussing how to market their wares in Africa, and I chatted with a student from Papua New Guinea who was studying at the nearby university. Gaziantep was knocking on the doors of the global economy, and it was joined by industrious Turkish cities across the Anatolian plateau.

Indeed, Turkey is rising, thanks to dizzying economic growth. Just a decade ago, the average Turk had one-fifth the income of the average European. Today, the Turks are only 30 percent less wealthy than EU citizens.[1] What is more, Turks have more purchasing power than some EU member country citizens, including Bulgarians, Romanians, and others.[2] Given Europe's financial doldrums, Turkey could catch up with Europe in the coming years and thus realize its four-centuries-old dream of becoming Western by catching up with the West.

Turkey's race with the West started soon after the Europeans crushed the Ottoman Empire's mighty army in Vienna in 1683—and "catching up" took many forms. During the Ottoman Empire's "Tulip Period" in the early eighteenth century, the sultans built gardens to emulate

Versailles and factories to mimic the industrial revolution, hoping to replicate Western Europe in Istanbul. In the late nineteenth century the Young Turks emerged to turn the Ottoman Empire into a constitutional monarchy, again following the European trends of the time. Mustafa Kemal Ataturk, the founder of the modern Turkish republic, too, followed Europe during the early part of the twentieth century. He turned to contemporary France for inspiration, striving to make Turkey a secular republic. Ataturk enshrined the new Turkish constitution with the principle of *laïcité*, that is, European secularism, mandating a firewall between religion and politics. In this project Ataturk had nearly complete political freedom; having liberated Turkey from Allied occupation at the end of World War I, the Turkish leader enjoyed immense clout and the backing of his military. In the second half of the twentieth century, Turkey joined NATO and became a multiparty democracy, anchoring itself in the West during the Cold War. Ankara also joined the Organisation for Economic Co-operation and Development (OECD) and launched itself on the path for EU membership, though that dream is yet to be fulfilled five decades after Turkey's application to join the union.

Turkey's catch-up game with the West and the ensuing experience with multiparty government brought the AKP, rooted in the country's Islamist movement, to power in Ankara in 2002. In the past decade under the AKP government Ataturk's *laïcité* model has largely collapsed in Turkey. Infused with deep religiosity, the AKP has all but eliminated the European-style firewall between religion and politics in Turkey, while continuing to pursue Turkey's long-held dream of catching up with the West in the economic sphere. Since 2002 Turkish economic output has nearly trebled.[3] Buoyed by this growth, Ankara has set its sights on joining the world's ten largest economies within a decade.[4] This aspiration speaks volumes about Turkey's grand ambitions. To attain this goal, Turkey would need to grow at over 8 percent annually.[5] Yet Turkey's leaders are unrelenting in setting this high bar, even as some experts argue that Turkey may hit the "middle income trap"[6] and will face difficulty moving up the income ladder with the same momentum as during the past decade.

The age-old Turkish dream of catching up with Europe appears nearer than ever before: Turkey recently joined the "trillion dollar plus" economies in Europe, providing Ankara with membership in an elite club of European economies including Germany, France, the United Kingdom, Italy, and Spain.

Can Turkey manage even more and become the twenty-first century's first Muslim power, achieving political clout in its neighborhood, and potentially across the world? And after a decade of rule by a party with an Islamist pedigree, what will remain of the country's Western political overlay, a major preoccupation for the sultans and Ataturk, alike? It all depends on how the political elites in the country's capital, Ankara, play their hands. Today Turkey faces a range of stress tests that will try its ability as a global actor as well as its commitments to Western interests and values. At the forefront of these challenges Turkey faces a crisis in Syria, where instability is spilling into Turkey and creating friction with Washington. Across the Arab world the rise of political Islam is both an opportunity for Turkey as well as a temptation that could lead Turkey to stray from its Western principles. Similarly Turkey's still fragile ties with Israel and its cold war with Cyprus are standing in the way of closer union with its Western neighbors. Navigating these challenges will determine Turkey's course in the years ahead.

In tackling these challenges, Turkey would do well to analyze the lessons of its impressive economic success over the last decade. Turkey has emerged as an economic powerhouse thanks to the successful blending of the country's traditional connections to European and other economies situated within the OECD with the dynamism of the emerging markets, especially Muslim majority societies in nearby nations. Turkish economic success since 2002 has rested on two premises. On the one hand Turkey has kept itself open to Europe, attracting significant investment from the continent.[7] On the other hand Turkey has simultaneously shifted its trade to the emerging markets and Muslim-majority countries to harness their growth. As late as 2007, 56 percent of Turkey's trade was with Europe. Today that figure is down to 42 percent.[8] In comparison its trade with the Middle East and North Africa has increased from 13 percent in 2002 to 26 percent today, and it continues to rise.[9] Meanwhile, Turkish trade with sub-Saharan Africa has gone from less than $1 billion annually in 2000 to over $17 billion.[10] This outreach has shaped Ankara's rise, both economically and politically. While the EU grew at an average 1.3 percent in the past decade, Turkey has grown at a whopping 5.3 percent.[11]

In other words Turkey has had the best of both worlds, simultaneously taking advantage of its proximity to Europe and its affinity with Muslim societies. This was made possible by a decade of unprecedented political stability provided by the AKP government. And international investors have taken notice. The major international rating agencies have upgraded Turkey within a hair's breadth of investment status.[12] However, by the same token this has come at the price of near single-party rule and growing authoritarianism since 2002.

Historically speaking, this might suggest an unsavory conclusion concerning the "Turkish model of success": the country's political system produces stability when dominated by a single-party government, and Turkey experiences political and economic spasms when ruled by coalitions. This is because, not unlike various other political cultures, Turkish elites tend to eschew a horizontal stratification of labor (a must for successful coalition governments) in favor of a hierarchical division that encourages single-party structures. Therefore Turkey has often faced political and economic meltdowns during periods of coalition government rule, as was the case in the 1970s and the 1990s. This pattern is especially evident when contrasted with the decades of political stability and economic growth in the 1950s under the Democrat Party (DP), 1980s under the Motherland Party (ANAP), and under the AKP period of single-party governance since 2002.

In the past decade, with the exception of the fourth quarter of 2008 and the year 2009,[13] the Turkish economy has grown during every quarter. Not only has Turkey become more prosperous, but this prosperity has arrived through a decade-long, nearly unbroken ascent. And all this while Turks have witnessed Europe, their historic benchmark, sputter in the wake of economic turmoil. No wonder then that the Turks today feel more confident about their relationship to Europe and the West than they have felt in decades. I witnessed this confidence first-

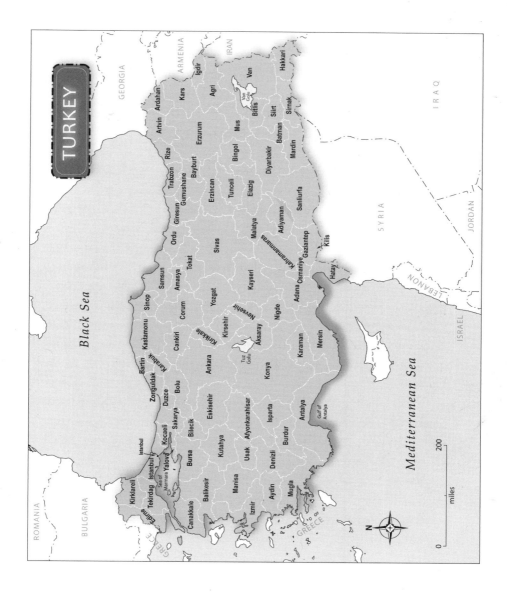

Map 1. Turkey with provinces and neighborhoods.
Courtesy of the Washington Institute for Near East Policy.

hand recently while chatting with a shopkeeper in the southern Turkish city of Adana, a town whose claim to fame is its fine cotton and the Incirlik Air Force Base, a hub of U.S. military operations in the Middle East. The shopkeeper told me that he had two uncles who had migrated to Germany in the 1980s and 1990s to seek jobs, but that he was not interested in following in their footsteps because, as he put it: "Turkey is so much better off than Europe now."

This confidence has been at the root of Turkey's recent foreign policy doctrine dubbed "strategic depth." Promoted by Ahmet Davutoglu, a demure, Turkish-Malaysian educated political scientist, the doctrine holds that it is time for Turkey to rise as a regional power. Professor Davutoglu explained this theory to back in 2004. At the time the AKP had just come to power, and only a few people in Washington had heard of Davutoglu or thought that the party would challenge Turkey's decades-old foreign policy strategy of aligning itself with U.S. views in the Middle East. "Turkey can become politically powerful again only if it utilizes the 'strategic depth' of its neighborhood, developing better ties with those Muslim neighbors," Davutoglu told me at his small office in downtown Ankara's ministerial quarter, a conglomeration of buildings from the interwar period providing for an awkward blend of Mussolini-chic and Ottoman-Turkish revival. "Turkey's future power depends on having good ties with its Muslim neighbors, especially nearby Iran and Syria."

And so, over the last decade Turkey shifted its Middle East policy to align itself closely with Syria and, to a lesser extent, Iran, only to find out that neither Damascus nor Tehran is Ankara's friend. The Syrian uprising, which Turkey supported almost from the beginning in 2011, has put Ankara at the opposing end of the Middle East spectrum in regards to the Bashar al-Assad regime and its regional patron, Tehran. Turkish tensions with Syria and Iran are serious concerns for Ankara. Damascus has allowed the Kurdistan Workers Party (PKK), which has been waging a war against Turkey since the 1970s, to operate inside Syria. When the Assad regime's hold over its territory weakened in summer 2012, the PKK and its Syrian affiliate Party for the Democratic Union Party (PYD) moved in to take over towns along the border with

Turkey. Ankara now has to deal with the prospect of PKK-controlled cantons in post-Assad Syria. Iran, too, has acted to retaliate against Turkey's Syria policy. In a successful attempt to punish Ankara, in September 2011 Tehran brokered a ceasefire with the Iranian branch of the PKK, the Party for a Free Life in Kurdistan (PJAK), against whom it had hitherto been fighting, allowing the group to focus its energy against Turkey. Iranian and Syrian support for the PKK is now a major threat for Ankara, but Turkey can turn the tables if it manages to sustain its peace talks with the PKK's imprisoned leader, Abdullah Ocalan, as well as reaching a final peace with its Kurds.

Still, these regional dynamics will continue to present a political challenge for the AKP and the ascendant Turkey it has governed. Until recently Davutoglu and the AKP found encouragement in Turkey's economic success and were emboldened to pursue an independent foreign policy, at times opposing the United States and breaking with Europe on Middle East issues such as Iran and Syria policy. In fact, though, Turkey's economic success harbors a very different lesson for the AKP: the country's economic miracle has been driven by a fine blend of political stability, European money, and access to emerging markets and Muslim-majority economies. If Ankara can now repeat this pattern in global politics—embracing its Muslim identity while providing political stability in its neighborhood, and at the same time maintaining strong ties with Europe, the United States, and other Western societies—this would truly deliver Turkey to the pantheon of global players. Such a foreign policy would make Turkey valuable for its neighbors to the east and west. This is because for the Muslim countries, Turkey's value lies in the fact that Turkey, while maintaining its Muslim character, has instilled its society and institutions with a Western overlay. And for the West, Turkey is valuable because it is a Muslim majority country that can act as a reliable partner.

Turkey can rise as a regional power only if brings added value to its Muslim neighbors. This means leveraging not just its Muslim identity but also its Western linkages as well. Accordingly, in September 2011 Turkey made the strategic choice to join NATO's missile defense project that aims to protect Alliance members against ballistic missiles launched from Iran and elsewhere, such as Russia and China. Setbacks like the break in Turkish-Israeli ties have tested Turkey's ability to strike this balance. But just as Turkey has come to realize the value of a relationship with Israel, it is increasingly coming to grasp a more basic truth about its destiny as a rising power: Turkey will rise as a cornerstone of regional stability only if Ankara can leverage its Muslim identity and Western overlay, maintaining its strong ties with the Western states even as it expands its influence as a Middle East power. For Turkey, this is the formula for global political greatness and the shortest path to international prominence not witnessed since the Ottoman armies challenged Europe at the gates of Vienna.

But this path is not smooth or certain. True, Turkey now rivals Indonesia for the designation of the world's largest Muslim-majority economy (and Indonesia has over three times Turkey's population). Likewise, Turkey has arguably the strongest conventional Muslim military force in the world.[14] But rampant instability on its borders and a perilous current account deficit could quickly send Turkey's global ascent into a downward spiral, especially if Turkey's leadership fails to heed the formula for Turkey's global rise.

Still, due to its sheer size, with 75 million citizens and a $1.3 trillion economy,[15] Turkey is better positioned than any other Muslim-majority country to potentially become the twenty-first century's first Muslim world power. In 2014 Turkey will take over the prestigious position as one of the executive directors of the International Monetary Fund (IMF)—a position that will come as further recognition of the country's newfound economic might.

Will these forces add up to lasting political greatness for Turkey, and what does all this mean for the United States? Turkey's growing prosperity and opening to the world places it in a category similar to the much discussed BRICS, but Turkey stands alone in several crucial respects as well: First, under the AKP Turkey has embraced its Muslim identity, setting it apart as a self-defined Muslim power. Second, Turkey has unique historical bonds with Europe and the United States, making its BRICS-like rise specifically relevant for the future course of Western power and institutions. Fortunately for the United States,

Turkey's rise will be indexed to its ability to reintegrate the Western international system. Turkey can only become the twenty-first century's first Muslim global power if it remains true to itself, synthesizing Islam and its Western overlay, the yin and yang of Turkishness since the days of the sultans.

The country has other challenges as well. Turkey's ascendance in the past decade has prompted Turkish policymakers to craft a new vision of their place in the world—a vision that reflects the deep societal shifts that have taken place under the leadership of its rather conservative AKP government. These shifts have meant the erosion of *laïcité*—much to the detriment of Turkey's secularists and liberals, who are concerned about the threat that government-backed social conservatism poses to individual liberties. Indeed, Turkey is split down the middle between AKP supporters and opponents. In the most recent 2011 elections, the governing party received 49.9 percent of the vote, indicating that the Turks are sharply divided over the role of religion in politics, whereas the 2013 Gezi park demonstrations paralyzed the country for months. Unless the country heals this split, it will be difficult for Ankara to realize its potential to become a global player. Political polarization could keep Turkey bogged down and looking inward. Turkey has to bring together its disparate social segments if it wants to emerge as a regional and global player, especially considering that the country is currently debating drafting its first-ever civilian-made constitution. If this new charter outlines the groundwork of true liberal democracy— for instance, providing for freedom of religion as well as freedom from religion—AKP supporters and opponents alike will be on their way to reconstituting a Turkey where individuals from all walks of life can thrive. A new social contract would, in return, enable Turkey to focus its energy overseas.

Indeed, by drafting a truly liberal charter, Turkey would be on its way to unlocking its potential in many areas. Not only would a new document provide space for the country's polarized ends to live together, but it would also allow Turkey to address its burning Kurdish problem. This is a challenge that has become even more pressing in recent years. The rise of Kurdish nationalism in Syria, Iraq, and Turkey sap Turkey's energy. Consequently Ankara has to find a solution to its Kurdish problem if it is to emerge as a regional player, free of domestic and regional violence that will consume the country's creative energy in foreign policy. As a fragile ceasefire process is underway, Turkey can consolidate its progress by providing for broader cultural and individual rights to all citizens, including but not specific to the Kurds, within the framework of the new constitution. This would be the most realistic remedy to Turkey's Kurdish problem. Such a formula within the new charter would likely satisfy both nationalist Kurds and also majority Turks who generally do not favor group-specific rights given to the Kurds.

Last but not least, a new charter would allow Turkey to emerge as a regional power by casting Turkey as a model for countries experiencing the Arab Spring. Only by serving as a shining example of liberal democracy—for instance, by drafting a constitution that guarantees freedom of speech broadly defined, equal political rights for Muslims and non-Muslims, as well as full gender equality—can Ankara promote itself as a source of inspiration for its Arab and Muslim majority neighbors. If, on the other hand, Turkey is a less-than-liberal democracy at home, it would be difficult for its Western partners to promote Ankara as a model for post–Arab Spring countries such as Egypt, Tunisia, Libya, and Yemen.

The AKP's worldview has at times been problematic in this respect. The party's grounding in Islamist politics informs Turkey's new impulse to carry the banner on causes that preoccupy other Sunni Muslim countries and can lead the Turks to take stands that challenge its partners in the West. But the new Turkey is not destined to become an irresponsible rising power. Ultimately, Turkey's new leaders are victims of their own success: The cornerstone of Turkey's rise has been the government's ability to foster stable political conditions for economic growth. Such policies have also helped the AKP win three successive elections, with increased majorities. The AKP has had an astounding electoral run, and its leadership wants to sustain this pattern in nationwide local elections, as well as presidential and parliamentary elections to be held in 2014 and 2015. This electoral success has been driven by phenomenal economic growth, which has, in return, been made possible by Turkey's image as a stable and regionally responsible country, a reputation that has benefitted Turkey by attracting record-breaking investments.

Accordingly, policies that could tarnish Turkey's reputation as a bastion of stability, such as failure to contain the fall-out of the Syrian war, risk sapping the very essence of Turkish power: its comparative stability in an uncertain region. This realization has been the catalyst for Ankara's recent careful balancing of East and West. Turkey's rapprochement with Israel and its convergence with NATO are two important consequences of this rebalancing.

What is more, rising Turkey will also face economic challenges. Kemal Dervis, the technocrat behind Turkey's economic transformation, which started with an IMF plan implemented in 2001, recently suggested that "Turkey is on its way to becoming a world economic powerhouse." Though Dervis also added that Turkey's "ascent will depend on how it manages challenges to its fiscal position and current account—and crucially, its ability to foster dialogue and compromise among its fractious politicians."[16]

In essence, Turkey's leaders need to realize that if Turkey is to become a global power, it must remain stable, bring together its disparate parts, and calibrate its rise within the Western international system. And Turkey must manage all this while continuing its outreach to the non-Western world. The result could be a new Turkey: a twenty-first-century Muslim power that is bound to promote stability, yet less restrained by a regional, European rubric. In other words, Turkey's age-old game of catch-up with Europe may be nearing its end, making way for a new Turkey that stands as a Muslim power with a place in the West.

1 | Turkey's New World

The Turks are selling pasta to the Italians, educating Papua–New Guineans in their own universities, building airports in Egypt, running schools in Nigeria, and establishing diplomatic missions in Latin America. Turkey has not felt this confident since the heyday of Ottoman imperial majesty in the sixteenth century—and it has started to move to a new stage in its catch-up game with the West.

As the Ottoman Empire slumped into decline in the eighteenth century, the Turks tried to join the European fold as a modern country, subsumed under the continent's political framework. That dream has likely passed. Over the past decade, however, a new Turkey has awakened, built by unprecedented political stability, domestic growth and commercial and political clout overseas. This sea change has instilled a sense of global confidence in the Turkish people not seen since Suleiman the Magnificent ruled in Constantinople. "And the new Turkey is here to stay," as Namik Tan, the Turkish ambassador to Washington, enthuses confidently. "Turkey feels like it has a world beyond Europe."

Like a Eurasian China, the new Turkey is interested in building influence across the globe and is no longer confined by a regional, European rubric. Gone are the days when Turkey waited humbly at the gates of Europe, shunning the vast expanse beyond its southern and eastern borders.

While visiting Istanbul just before the Syrian uprising broke out in

March 2011, I attended a conference on the Arab Spring organized by the Abant Platform, a local nongovernmental organization (NGO) linked to the prestigious Gulen Movement, led by Fethullah Gulen, that gathers Turkish intellectuals of different stripes for policy debates. The conference—this time with attendees from Washington, Tel Aviv, London, St. Petersburg, and Arab capitals, in addition to Turks—debated Turkey's leadership role in the Arab Spring.

The venue was Ciragan Palace, a former Ottoman residence on the Bosporus and an apt selection for the new Turkey. Over Turkish coffee served à la Ottoman with double-roasted Turkish delight on the side, Ali Aslan, a Turkish journalist, summed up the new Turkey for me: "Ten years ago, the Turks would not have organized a conference on the Middle East lest this make them look non-European. And if such a conference were ever conceived, it would be run by the government and staged in Ankara, with all the participants making arguments in favor of following Europe's footsteps."

IT'S THE ECONOMY . . .

The Turks are becoming ever more self-assured as the world around them is stricken with a crisis of confidence from economic meltdown. Meanwhile, Turkey has been booming: its economy roared forward in 2011, growing at a rate of over 13 percent in the first quarter and nearly 9 percent in the second,[1] outpacing not only its neighbors but also all of Europe. During the first six months of 2011 Turkey even vied with China for position as the world's fastest growing economy.[2] Since 2002 the Turkish economy has nearly tripled in size, experiencing the longest spurt of prosperity in modern Turkish history. The Turkish daily *Cumhuriyet* wrote that in 2011 alone another 9,755 millionaires joined the country's wealthy, and per capita income has more than doubled over the past decade, when measured in Purchasing Power Parity (PPP).[3] Just as the sudden spread of middle-class prosperity in the United States in the 1950s instilled a can-do attitude in American sentiment toward the world, the same is now happening in Turkey. A young Kurdish cab driver from Istanbul's poorer outer districts, whom I met while taking a cab across the Golden Horn, said proudly: "Europe is too small an arena for Turkey; we need to be a global player."

In fact, Turkey is well on its way to becoming just that. Turkey's trade with the world has gone from $82 billion in 2000 to over $389 billion in 2012,[4] and the sheer increase in volume has been complimented by an expanding scope: Turkey is selling more products to a more diverse array of countries. Early last decade Turkey cut its teeth in the global marketplace selling unfinished or simple products to untapped markets in its neighborhood. Companies originating in Anatolia (the country's rural, conservative heartland also known as Asia Minor), like the snack maker Ulker, conquered store shelves in the Middle East, recently acquiring Godiva chocolates. Meanwhile, Istanbul-based manufacturers became a force to be reckoned with; for instance, Pasabahce, a glass manufacturer that finds inspiration in Ottoman-era glassmaking, has become a top seller, dominating the markets across Eastern Europe and the Middle East.[5] And now Turkey is moving up the value chain, clawing its way toward the towering heights of global trade in high-tech sectors.

Turkey is putting its weight behind this effort more than ever before; the share of funds allocated to research and development has more than doubled its share in Turkey's gross domestic product (GDP) since 2004—and lean, dynamic firms are at the head of this drive, finding markets and battling for position across the global marketplace. Take, for example, Mutlu Batteries, a midsized company that operates on the outskirts of Istanbul and has become the biggest manufacturer of batteries in Eastern Europe and the Middle East.[6] Turkey is even trying its hand at the PC business. Casper, a firm started in 1991 by three Turkish engineers, has grown into a regionally advertised technology firm that can produce as many as one million PCs per year for sale in Turkey, Europe, and the Middle East.[7] But perhaps the greatest source of pride for Turks in the last decade is the burgeoning auto industry. Turkey's state planners had been trying to foster a Turkish automobile manufacturing base since the 1950s, but in the end it was integration with the global economy and accession to the EU's customs union in 1995 that kick-started Turkey's dreams of building competitive cars.

Over the past decade Turkey's automotive sector has grown in leaps and bounds, thanks to partnerships with leading firms such as Ford, Renault, and Fiat.[8] In 2011 Turkey's top export category was automobiles,[9] and Turkey ranked seventeenth among car-exporting countries.

To find buyers for this burst of productive energy, Turkey has branched out beyond its old markets in Europe. The continent's economic doldrums coupled with Turkey's new trans-European vision means that the country's traditional commercial bonds with Europe are plateauing while its trade links with the non-European world flourish. In 1999, for instance, the EU accounted for over 56 percent of Turkish trade. In 2011 this number went down to 41 percent, while the share of members of the Organization of Islamic Cooperation (OIC) in Turkish trade climbed from 12 percent to 20 percent in the same period. Over the past decade Turkish diplomats have gone on a veritable spree of initiating free trade agreements (FTAs), signing agreements with Albania, Bosnia-Herzegovina, Chile, Croatia, Egypt, Georgia, Jordan, Lebanon, Montenegro, Morocco, the Palestinian Authority, the Republic of Korea, Serbia, Syria, and Tunisia. Turkey's voracious appetite for international trade seems to have few limits; in 2011 Turkey even signed an FTA with the Republic of Mauritius, a tiny island off the coast of Madagascar, boosting its trade volume with the island to over $51 million,[10] a substantial amount of money for an island with a GDP of only about $11 billion.

Indeed, Turkey's trade expansion has shown a sharp turn toward new and nontraditional markets. In the year 2000 about 9 percent of Turkey's $27 billion worth of exports went to the Middle East. By 2011 Turkey's total exports had risen to $134 billion, and exports to the Middle East had grown sharply ahead of the curve, constituting 20 percent of this value. Turks are selling more to Russia and Eastern Europe as well. Turkish exports to Poland are nine times greater than in 2000, and Turkey's exports to Moldova are eight times greater. Turkey has also increased its exports to Russia eightfold, not to mention the role that Turkish construction firms have played in the construction of post-Soviet Russia. The country's traders are even making inroads in more remote destinations, such as sub-Saharan Africa. In 2000 about

1 percent of Turkey's exports went to these countries. Today this percentage has jumped to 2.6 percent, marking a twelvefold increase in exports to these countries.[11] Areas that once seemed far-flung to Turkish entrepreneurs are now becoming prime targets. In the past decade Turkey's exports to Afghanistan have gone from a measly $8 million to over $275 million, and its exports to Morocco have risen no less than thirteen fold.[12] From Beirut to Brunei, the Turkish trading state is energetically looking to break into markets around the world, and Turkey's upper and middle classes are reaping the rewards.

The downside of this trend is Turkey's growing dependence on costly energy exports to feed its productive appetites. Soaring trade volumes with Russia and Iran are largely the result of expensive natural gas and energy imports, putting a crater-sized dent in Turkey's trade balance. In response the government has made energy diversification a priority. This will be one of Turkey's main economic challenges: becoming less dependent on Russia and Iran for oil and gas imports by diversifying energy import markets while becoming more energy efficient. Otherwise, Ankara's economic growth could be unexpectedly stunted by political problems with Tehran and Moscow. And Ankara's ties with both states have been rocky lately due to the crisis in Syria. The risk looms of a potential spike in energy prices due to regional conflict, such as an Israeli strike on Iranian nuclear facilities.

Paralleling this trend of diversification of trade partners, Turkey's ruling AKP has pursued a foreign policy that transcends Ankara's European vocation, irreversibly remolding Turkey's identity. Yet these tectonic shifts have been accompanied by a governing mentality that prioritizes stability above all else: "After suffering through eight coalition governments and four economic crises, the Turkish people have welcomed ten years of a stable AKP government even if it has meant entrenched single-party rule," says Asli Aydintasbas, a columnist with mainstream Turkish daily *Milliyet*. Indeed, stability has been the watchword for political success in Turkey. In early 2012 Turks were polled on their voting preferences. When asked why they voted for the AKP, the largest number (25 percent) of Turks cited its ability to bring stability (the second most popular answer was admiration for the AKP's charismatic leader, Prime Minister Erdogan).[13] The international economy has likewise cast its vote in favor of political stability. Turkey is a comparative underperformer when it comes to attracting foreign direct investment (FDI), and its economic leaders often complain that Turkey gets a bad rap from international credit-rating agencies. However, thanks to stable political conditions and an improving investment climate, this trend is reversing. Turkey has tamed its public finances over the past decade, bringing its debt-to-GDP ratio down from 62 percent in 2003 to 49 percent in 2011 and 37 percent in 2013.[14] Turkey has also nearly finished paying its debts to the IMF, which it incurred during its 2001 financial crisis. The AKP government has won additional plaudits for its economic governance due to its steady, though imperfect, regulatory approach. As a result Turkey is increasingly becoming a destination for international capital. In 2003 FDI inflows to Turkey stood at only $1.8 billion. By 2012 this figure had grown to nearly $16 billion;[15] Turkey has overhauled its commercial law and has designed a suite of investment incentive packages in the hopes of drawing ever greater volumes of FDI in the coming decade.

Elected in 2002 and slated to pick the country's next president in 2014, the AKP has already run Turkey longer than any other party since Ankara became a democracy in 1946. As it is likely to outlive even Ataturk's fifteen-year domination of Turkish politics in the early twentieth century, the AKP's global vision is likely to prevail.

AND THE ANATOLIAN TIGERS

Buoyed by economic dynamism, political stability, and a new supra-European vision, the Turks have accordingly reached far and wide to build soft power in places they had earlier ignored, such as the Middle East, Africa, and even far-flung countries like Vietnam and Mongolia.

The private sector, universities, and NGOs are driving this agenda, shaping the new Turkish supra-European identity. This trend can best be observed in cities dominated by the middle class in Gaziantep, the country's sixth largest city, as well as in other middle-sized cities such as Kayseri, Konya, Malatya, and Denizli. Dubbed "the Anatolian Tigers" for driving the country's record-breaking growth rate, these towns have also provided solid support to the AKP while linking Turkey to the Middle East, Africa, and beyond.

Gaziantep, near the Syrian border, has factories that manufacture a plethora of goods, selling products to over seventy countries. The town's pasta ends up on Italian dinner plates. In this sense, Gaziantep is like an Anatolian Guangzhou, the Chinese hub famous for selling its wares to the most distant and unlikely places.

But unlike Guangzhou, Gaziantep is also building soft power for Turkey. The area's Zirve University is a testament to this. Funded by the local billionaire Nakiboglu family, which made its wealth recently in international commerce, the new university has a gleaming campus that rises amid Gaziantep's famous pistachio groves.

Visiting this campus is like visiting the new Turkey. Gokhan Bacik, a professor of international relations who studies Turkey's new active Middle East policy, told me that already over 10 percent of the university's student body is foreign, despite the fact that the university opened only two years ago. Many students hail from the Middle East, especially nearby Syria, as well as the Balkans, Africa, the former Soviet Union, and even Western Europe. "We have students from Austria and Papua New Guinea," he added.

Gaziantep is the epitome of the new Turkey. For years it was known in Turkey for its heavenly baklava. Today, shops in the town's gentrifying old city and along tram-lined streets in leafy middle-class districts proudly display signs promoting "the world's best baklava," making a culinary claim to Turkey's new global identity. Yet, there is also another Gaziantep in the making. Businesspeople from this city and other Anatolian Tigers are busy financing and managing construction projects across the world, including Cairo's new airport terminal and major projects from Russia to Mongolia. Others are launching schools to educate future elites in countries around the globe, including Nigeria, Morocco, Brazil, and Vietnam, demonstrating further soft power in the making. Most of these businessmen and schools belong to the Sufi-inspired Gulen Movement, a force to be reckoned with in the new Turkey. Mustafa Sungur, who sympathizes with the movement, says, "The Movement has Turkish schools in almost all countries of the world with the exception of authoritarian places such as North Korea, Iran, and Saudi Arabia."

Gaziantep also demonstrates that the blend of capitalism in the new Turkey can lead to cosmopolitanism, a welcome development. In the twentieth century before the Ottoman Empire collapsed, Gaziantep was a multiethnic city in which Armenians and Jews lived with Muslim Turks around a medieval citadel. Though a satellite city to the much larger Aleppo (under whose political authority Gaziantep fell), the city, known as Ayintab to the Ottomans, had a cosmopolitan outlook, with an American College and an Armenian Catholic Church. The city's Armenian population all but disappeared during the calamities of World War I, and the smaller Jewish community migrated to Istanbul and later to Israel during the "terrible 1970s" when Turkey suffered its worst economic and political problems since the founding of the republic in 1923.

Gaziantep's economic rise has been a story of the city's restoration of its multiethnic past, as well as a claim to a cosmopolitan identity. Just as Gaziantep's economy began to pick up speed in 2000, a massive trove of mosaics and ancient artifacts were discovered near the archeological site of Zeugma, a settlement that dates back to Alexander the Great's conquests. The city's newly moneyed elite rallied behind the efforts to salvage the mosaics of Zeugma, establishing a world-class museum on the premises of a defunct tobacco factory. The Zeugma Museum, an iconic building with a twenty-three-thousand-square-foot exhibition space and some of the most impressive Roman mosaics found to date, is a symbol of the new Gaziantep. The museum attracts tourists from such far-flung countries as Japan and Venezuela; in 2011 alone sixty thousand people visited it. Gaziantep's success in creating a museum to host classical-era art and hence put itself on the world map is a case of successful marriage between capitalism and the new Turkey.

The city's claim to a cosmopolitan identity through the discovery of its past can also be observed in the town's citadel district, the core of historic Gaziantep. In the past decade the local government has used EU funds to restore the old city, starting a process of gentrification in the city's historic hub, including its synagogue and churches. In the past years the city government has restored the Armenian Surp Bedros Church, which was long buried under rubble after its destruction during World War I and the ensuing Ottoman collapse, making this the first Armenian church in modern Turkey to rise from its ashes since the demise of the Ottoman Empire. Currently, the local government is also restoring the dilapidated Antep Synagogue, another first for a Jewish site in modern Turkey.

In addition, the old city now features smartly refurbished Mamelukestyle mosques, outdoor markets and bazaars, boutique hotels in nineteenth-century mansions, organic food stores, restaurants that attract diners on "gourmet tours" from Istanbul, and private museums, including one that exhibits local glassware and another that showcases Gaziantep's famed cuisine.

One of the restored market places is Zeytin Han, a medieval marketplace that now serves as an emporium for fine olive oils and fancy soaps. But perhaps no Gaziantep establishment measures up to the renowned baklava maker Imam Cagdas, a bakery dating from the Ottoman-era that attracts Turks all the way from Istanbul and produces over 2.5 tons of baklava per day. This economic vibrancy, in turn, has enabled greater support for reviving Gaziantep's cultural richness. For example, the Zeugma restoration project is made possible in part by the local chamber of commerce and various NGOs supported by local donors.

In the end Turkey's newfound economic dynamism, creative energy, and cosmopolitan identity, as epitomized by the new Gaziantep, all point to the old imperial capital of Istanbul. By securing itself in the Middle East, the former Soviet Union, Asia, and Africa, the new Turkey is anchoring these regions in Istanbul. Once the center of the Ottoman, Byzantine, and Roman Empires, Istanbul is once again reclaiming its dominance as a global capital. Accounting for over one-third of Turkey's $1.3 trillion economy, Istanbul's wealth already dwarfs all of Turkey's neighbors, except for oil-rich Iran. A banker friend of mine in Istanbul says that the city is so wealthy that "you could fit all of Austria in it, and there would still be space economically for a few small European countries to be thrown in."

Yet Istanbul reaches even beyond Turkey's immediate neighbors. Ten years ago one could fly direct from Istanbul to a mere seventy-five international destinations, most of them in Europe, on Turkish Airlines, the country's flagship carrier. Today Turkish Airlines offers direct flights from Istanbul to more than two hundred international destinations.[16] The majority of the new destinations are in Africa, the Middle East, and Asia, including Dhaka, Dar es Salam, and Damman. In Iraq alone the airline serves six cities, providing the most international connections with that country of any airline, and in December 2011 the company provided the first international connection to Misrata, Libya, beating the competition to reach Libya's newly accessible oil capital, as well as launching the first direct flight from the Middle East to San Paulo.

Turkey's new global identity is increasingly shaping its foreign policy, as well. Like the country's national airlines, its diplomats seem to be following Turkey's businesspeople and reaching even further. In the past decade Turkey has opened up over forty new diplomatic missions, most of them in Africa and Asia, including Basra, Maputo, Accra, Juba, and Yaoundé. It has also set up posts in Latin America and now has diplomatic reach in Bogota and Santiago.

This posturing suggests that Turkey's new supra-European identity and global confidence are here to stay. That, of course, requires the Turkish economy to keep humming and the country to remain stable. If Turkey plays its hand well, the same economic factors responsible for facilitating its rise beyond Europe will help it maintain its confident global outlook.

DEMOGRAPHY AND THE PROMISE OF VAROS

Turkey's rise also depends on how it manages its current demographic transformation. Between 1960 and 2000 the Turkish population experienced a boom, increasing from 28 million to nearly 67 million. Since the mid-1990s the country's population growth rate has stabilized and then declined. In 1999 Turkey's fertility rate dropped and it now stands at 2.1, just the rate needed for any society to replenish its population.[17]

In other words, Turkey's population, which stands at 75 million, is no longer booming. However, at the same time, the country's population is increasing in age. This presents both an opportunity and a challenge for Turkey.

The AKP has been lucky in the sense that it came to power soon after Turkey's population growth rate stabilized, with the bulk of the population forming a young yet mature and productive bloc. After a country undergoes a population boom, its young population eventually matures to the point that the majority of the populace falls within the fifteen to sixty-four age group. This phenomenon, known as the "demographic window," drives creativity and dynamism. Provided there is good governance, it also delivers miraculous economic growth. Take, for instance, South Korea, which entered its demographic window in the 1980s, giving it the momentum in its leap out of poverty and into First World standards of productivity, with income levels matching those of Japan.

Still, Turkey's recent population growth also presents a challenge: massive migration from rural areas to cities. In 1960 only 32 percent of the Turks lived in cities. In 2011 this number had climbed up to 71 percent. This urbanization is likely to continue until around 90 percent of the Turks become urban, fitting into the pattern of other industrialized societies. Turkey's population is projected to reach 85.4 million in 2025, which suggests that in the following decade, Turkey will need to create room for over 20 million people in already crowded cities.[18] Gaziantep is a perfect place to observe the challenges of this process. To the west of this city's prosperous downtown lies Ibrahimli, a middle-class neighborhood with gleaming private schools, tree-lined streets, and cafes serving New York–style cheesecakes and sushi. To the south a new Gaziantep is emerging near the campus of Zirve University, populated by million-dollar villas, encircling a man-made pool large enough to accommodate sailboats. Not just Turks, but also wealthy Syrians who want to safeguard their money from that country's unrest, are buying homes in the rising Kucukkizilhisar district in the hills overlooking olive groves and Syria in the distance.

Yet there is also another Gaziantep, to the north and east of the city's downtown area. Meet Karsiyaka (in Turkish, "the other side"), a vast, poor, and mostly Kurdish neighborhood—the other half of Gaziantep. The Turks call districts such as Karsiyaka varos. Borrowed from Hungarian during Ottoman rule over Budapest in the seventeenth century, the word varos, which means "city" in Hungarian, means something quite different in contemporary Turkish, standing for poor, outlying districts of large cities. In the Karsikaya varos, rural migrants eke out a living doing menial tasks, such as cracking walnuts by hand in their homes.

In the past decade the AKP has done well in varos like Karsiyaka, taking advantage of its grassroots power base. This approach was made possible by the political vacuum left after a military coup in 1980 broke the leftist and labor movements that once held sway in such working-class neighborhoods. The AKP's predecessor, RP, often known as the Welfare Party, filled the gap, making its biggest gains among recent immigrants to the varos, a group that now forms Turkey's demographic plurality. Drawing on its Welfare Party roots, the AKP inherited the votes of the varos constituency, and the AKP's social policies resonated with the many millions of internal migrants looking for a better life in the cities while holding fast to their socially conservative values.

The varos were not attracted to the established and socially liberal center-right secular political parties, such as True Path Party (DYP) and the Motherland Party (ANAP). And with no leftist working-class parties in sight after the debilitating effect of the 1980 coup on the Turkish left, this population in the varos turned to the socially conservative Welfare Party. When that party was banned by Turkey's supreme court for being Islamist in 1998, after a brief hiatus these voters turned to its successor, the AKP in 2002. The Welfare Party's existing networks in the varos, which the AKP inherited, came in handy during its rise to power. Since then Chicago-style patron-client networks (doling out jobs and contracts in return for political support) and shared, mutually reinforced social conservatism have made the varos and the AKP partners in running Turkey.

The AKP has also used its decade in power to construct a functioning welfare system in Turkey that makes perceptible improvements in the lives of the varos dwellers. A prime example is the healthcare "green card" program that the AKP has expanded, offering public and private health services to low-income individuals at no cost. Today the AKP garners strong support in the varos. The party has a comparative advantage in this regard: its leader and Turkish prime minister Erdogan is himself from Kasimpasa, a tough, low-income varos neighborhood in Istanbul. Erdogan's success resides in his ability to effortlessly resonate with the plurality of Turks.

All this has helped the AKP win major victories, through solid support in the varos. The 2009 local elections and the 2011 general elections demonstrated this pattern across the country. In Istanbul the main opposition Republican People's Party (CHP) won victories in the middle and upper-middle classes, and long established districts like Besiktas, Sariyer, and Kadikoy, where luxurious houses overlooking the Bosporus line avenues of high-class shopping and fine dining, as well as apartment blocks for middle-class Turks. The AKP, on the other hand, made its strongest showing in the outlying varos neighborhoods far from Istanbul's fabulous wealth, winning in the working-class districts of Gungoren, Esenyurt, and Bagcilar, for example.

Ankara showed the same divisions. The CHP captured the high-income district of Cankaya and the wealthy areas in Yenimahalle, a middle-class commuter suburb west of Ankara connected to the city's downtown through subway lines, while the AKP maintained its stronghold in the low-income districts, such as Sincan and Altindag. Demographic trends suggest that this political pattern has played out well for the AKP. Continued migration to the cities means that the urban varos populations grow much more quickly than the established city dwellers who vote CHP, putting a growing voter base behind the AKP.

The varos helped make the AKP. Still, the varos presents the AKP and Turkey a demographic challenge: creating enough jobs and opportunities for the growing number of varos residents. If the AKP continues to keep the varos happy, it will likely win Turkey's next elections, and the country will continue to grow.

Yet another challenge for the AKP is the country's current accounts deficit, which ballooned to 9.8 percent in 2011, the highest figure among the forty-two developed economies recently reviewed by the *Economist*. By curbing its growth rate, Turkey managed to tame its account deficit in 2012, but as Turkey's economy accelerates again, so does its looming account gap. Most economies cannot sustain such a high deficit, but Turkey has been able to manage due to its position of stability amongst its neighbors, which has convinced investors to finance its deficit with massive portfolio inflows, at least for now.

My brother, Ali Cagatay, Bloomberg Turkey's news editor, told me that as much as $6 billion flowed into Turkey from Iran, Iraq, Syria, Lebanon, and the former Soviet Union in the first ten months of 2011 alone, helping the country's economy finance its deficit. In Turkey's Hatay province, which borders Syria, bank deposits increased by $1.1 billion in 2011, thanks to wealthy Syrians safeguarding their money in Turkey. Between 2010 and 2012 Hatay bank deposits rose by 33.7 percent.[19] In addition to money coming in from its non-European neighbors, Turkey also attracts massive inflows from European and other Western banks, which see Turkish markets as a "rare safe haven in these tumultuous times," adds a Turkish banker based in London.

This is why it is essential that the new Turkey be a responsible global player. Take, for instance, Ankara's threats to Israel over the flotilla incident. After Israel refused to apologize, some officials threatened to send the Turkish navy to confront the Israelis. But this option was never really on the table. As Turkey's leaders no doubt understand, it is in Turkey's best interest to avoid conflict, which is the reason Ankara backed down from the confrontation, and ultimately began to patch-up ties with the Israelis. Indeed, in spring 2011, when a Turkish NGO approached Ankara to send a "second flotilla" to Israel on the anniversary of the first flotilla, Ankara refused to allow this, reportedly as per Washington's request. Finally, in March 2013 Washington facilitated a breakthrough between Erdogan and Netanyahu, restoring diplomatic ties between the pair.

Here is how Turkey's foreign policy will look in the coming years: Turkey is confident and can afford to look beyond Europe as it continues to grow. And Turkey grows because it is deemed stable while the world around it convulses politically and economically. An aggressive foreign policy and political instability would court economic disaster, ending Turkey's bid for global influence. In short, the new Turkey's soft power rests on Turkey having a soft touch, politically.

2 | Conservative Islam Meets Capitalism

Kayseri, once known by its Roman name, Caesarea, is a central Anatolian boomtown flanked by the Anatolian plateau to the north and the Erciyes volcano to the south, an inactive, Fuji-like majestic peak that stands 12,848 feet tall. Lying at the intersection of this stark geological juxtaposition, Kayseri is a living example of Turkey's new synthesis of capitalism and Islam.

Kayseri is a prosperous city with a strong, recently developed export-oriented industrial base—in other words, an Anatolian Tiger like Gaziantep. In 2000 the town's population was only 690,000.[1] Today, it stands at over one million. This stunning growth, just as in Gaziantep, is due to Kayseri's opening up to the global economy. Today Kayseri exports furniture, textiles, and electronics, such as Ethernet cords and fiber-optic cables, to over 145 countries, from Russia to the United States, and even to Ecuador.[2] In 2011 the city's exports totaled $1.5 billion, equaling over $1,400 for each Caesarean citizen.

Like Gaziantep, Kayseri is a well-managed and even better-looking midsized Turkish city; it has a recently minted tram network and a world-class soccer arena, which the Union of European Football Association (UEFA) ranks on par with Barcelona's famous Camp Nou. Kayseri has four universities, three of them established in the last decade. In fact, Kayseri appears more modern and wealthy than Gaziantep, which is ringed by poor, mostly Kurdish neighborhoods. Abject poverty is all but non-existent in Kayseri, which also has much better infrastructure.

While Gaziantep is dynamic, yet rough around the edges, Kayseri is as pristine (almost sterile) a city as any traveler to Turkey can expect to encounter. Yet, unlike Gaziantep, Kayseri is hardly a hub of cosmopolitan diversity. The city does not have Gaziantep-like cultural facilities, nor does it seem to be rushing to embrace its non-Muslim past.

Whereas Gaziantep stands as an example of how the blend of capitalism and the new Turkey can lead to economic growth and cosmopolitanism, Kayseri paints a different picture. Until the collapse of the Ottoman Empire, Kayseri, like Gaziantep, was a multiconfessional city. Although a majority of Ottoman Kayseri's citizens were Turkish Muslims, the city was also home to large communities of Gregorian Armenians and Turkish-speaking Greek Orthodox Christians known as Karamanlis.[3] Today, Kayseri is home to only a small Armenian community. Though the Armenian community has recently refurbished the Surp Krikor Lusavoric church,[4] there is little in the new Kayseri that reminds the visitor of the city's once vibrant multi-religious past. The town has no internationally renowned cultural institutions like the Zeugma Museum in Gaziantep, nor is it making a visible attempt to engage with global culture. In other words Kayseri appears to be a capitalist success story, but without the colorful cosmopolitan or liberal political accompaniments. Perhaps this is best symbolized by the fact that while Gaziantep's claim to fame is the citizen-built Zeugma Museum that attracts visitors from as far abroad as Japan and California, Kayseri's main attraction is the Kadir Has soccer arena, a state-of-the-art facility catering to the billion-dollar soccer industry in Turkey.

In essence Kayseri is a money-making but not-quite-liberal Anatolian Tiger; it is where capitalism meets conservative Islam, each fortifying the other. Travelers to Kayseri looking for a nightcap will take notice of this right away: it is nearly impossible to find an establishment that serves alcohol in the city. There is a certain irony in the fact that a city that can support many international businesses and fine hotels, including a deluxe Hilton, lacks any establishments that serve liquor, the consumption of which is considered a sin by some Muslims affiliated with orthodox interpretations of Islam. The prosperous town is open for business but not for a liberal urban lifestyle, a carnival of capitalism without the color. This dramatic juxta-position of twenty-first-century economics and conservative austerity showcases an important aspect of Turkey's transformation under the leadership of the AKP and Erdogan. Just as Mustafa Kemal Ataturk came to embody the secular, Western character of the Turkish state, Erdogan is at the forefront of Islam's revival in the public sphere. A number of Muslim-majority nations have fused tradition with modern markets to climb the economic ladder in recent decades. Indonesia, for example, has unlocked market forces to raise millions out of pov-erty in the short span of a generation. Yet Turkey presents the most mature synthesis of markets and Islam by going even further in for-mulating a new brand of social conservatism that is often sanctioned by the government and self-imposed by the business community. This ethos equates economic virtue with religiosity, much like traditional Calvinism, where piety and industriousness made up two sides of the same coin. Also, like Europe's early moderns, this emerging conser-vative social order carries with it an exacting moral code that leaves little room for the personal sphere of privacy and individual choice that liberals so zealously guard.

GOVERNMENT-SANCTIONED SOCIAL CONSERVATISM

For many years the issue of secularism versus Islam has been an impor-tant and politically divisive issue in Turkey. One can trace the issue back to the nineteenth century when the Ottoman Empire initiated Western-oriented reforms, leading to a period when the public was divided into perceived Islamists and Westerners.

The establishment of the Turkish Republic ended this division when it officially codified Westernization by enacting a series of reforms to secularize not only the state but also the society at large (a first for a Muslim country and a definite setback for Islamists). According to the republic's founding fathers, the West represented the civilized world, and progress meant leaving traditionalism and public religiosity behind. Although the republic's early legislation discriminated against Islamists, this attitude eased somewhat with the transition away from one-party politics in the 1950s. After that, various political parties began to heed Islamic sensibilities in order to broaden their electoral base.

With the emergence of Islamist political parties in the late 1960s and the early 1970s, Islamists and secularists both learned valuable lessons. Realizing the impossibility of an Islamic state in Turkey, Islamists abandoned their demand for *sharia* (Islamic law). Over the years Islamist parties moderated their discourse, and today even some of the most radical groups recognize that Turkey will remain somehow secular. Hakan Yavuz, a scholar of Turkish Islam, describes Islam's unique position in Turkey society:

> Many Turks want to see Islam play a role in the public sphere but there is almost no support for the implementation of sharia. Turkey is more Islamic today than several decades earlier, but the support for sharia implementation has declined even as the public has become more pious. As a result of the consolidation of state power and the booming economy, Islam in Turkey has become bonding, not binding: a religion reduced to a moral code without legal obligations.[5]

The main issue today is the conservative Islamization of Turkish society, a scenario that until the AKP came to power most secular Turks thought was out of the question. Although Islamist parties were kept out of political power for many years, religion has always been an integral part of Turkish life, even during Turkey's most radical republican period. Islamic holidays, for instance, were always observed as national holidays.

If Turkey has, strictly speaking, not become more religious over the past decade, it certainly appears to have become more conservative, and going against this grain can now come with a social toll, especially outside of cosmopolitan settings. Binnaz Toprak, an Istanbul-based sociologist, conducted studies in 1999 and 2006, asking Turks about the connection between religion and discrimination in society. In 1999 some 47 percent of respondents reported discrimination in some form, with the official ban on Islamic-style headscarves in universities playing a large role in this perception. In 2006, however, this figure dropped to

17 percent. The AKP's rise seemingly reduced the level of discrimination felt by religious and conservative Turks.[6]

While Toprak's previous work argued that secularists were responsible for isolating Islamic groups from mainstream society, her more recent studies show the opposite could be true: rising social conservatism is creating an environment of discrimination against secular and liberal Turks, particularly women. In 2009 Toprak and her team interviewed 401 people from twelve different Turkish cities, including individuals from the lower-middle-class districts of Istanbul where the AKP is popular. Although the surveyed group was relatively small and not necessarily a representative sample, individuals from different regions voiced similar stories and patterns of discrimination. For example, uncovered female nurses and doctors from across the country reported being assigned to night shifts, while their colleagues who covered their heads in the Islamic fashion were given day shifts.[7]

In a different case of government-led discrimination, an Alevi doctor from a public hospital stated that before the AKP came to power, approximately 178 Alevi doctors worked at a particular hospital; now the number was only 3.[8] Some teachers in Turkey's public schools have even been accused of promoting these prejudices. For example, an Alevi student told Toprak's research team that when he approached a teacher to inquire why he scored lower than expected on an exam, the teacher ridiculed him in front of the class—calling him a "dirty Alevi"— and adding that given his background, he should be happy just to be attending the class.[9]

RISING SOCIAL CONSERVATISM AND INTOLERANCE

For several reasons Binnaz Toprak's study sheds light on the new Turkey that the AKP is molding. First, for many years people have defined conservative Turks in terms of the "other," a marginalized group facing discrimination. Toprak's study suggests that Turkey may be witnessing the inception of the *"other-other,"* constituted by liberal and secular Turks outside the middle-class neighborhoods of big cities who now face discrimination by the government's bureaucrats and employees.

Second, research shows that government-appointed bureaucrats use signs of social conservatism, such as the wearing of headscarves and disdain for alcohol, as benchmarks for making appointments and promotions and handing out government contracts. Since no legal or administrative recourse exists (such as an ombudsman) for people who face such government discrimination, most Turks feel that to succeed they need at least to act conservative. In other words it is not necessarily religiosity that is ascendant in Turkey, but rather social conservatism. However, the problem is not social conservatism per se, but government-imposed social conservatism, an idea that, among other things, is incompatible with a European Turkey. In this regard outward signs of social conservatism are gaining strength, since many Turks feel the need to blend in with Turkey's new social norms and curry favor with government officials.

Third, Turkey has always had a strong tradition of social conservatism. But while earlier bureaucrats and teachers would not have expressed prejudice toward liberals, women, and secular Muslims for fear of disciplinary action, discrimination is now practiced openly. Accordingly, because the state bureaucracy is imposing on Turkish society its idea of what constitutes a "good Muslim," intolerance is on the rise.

KEY TO THE AKP'S SUCCESS: BETTER LIVES

Why do so many Turks support the AKP's conservative agenda? Politically Turkey has undergone a complete transformation since 2002: The AKP has won three consecutive elections, with increasing majorities. The party, representing a brand of Islamic social conservatism, has replaced Turkey's former secularist elites. Once in power, the party pursued a policy that delivered phenomenal economic growth. It thereby became so popular that it was able to reshape Turkey, bringing the once-dominant military under its control as well as Turkey's elites—including the staunchly secular courts, business community, and the media—into its camp. In short the AKP's success story is more about economic policies than culture wars. When the AKP first presented voters with its party platform in 2002, it devoted the lion's share of its attention to the economy. In the ninety-page 2002 election manifesto more than thirty-five pages are devoted solely to the AKP's plans for economic development.[10]

The AKP has built political support for its platform by making significant improvements to the lives of common Turks. Turkey has indeed come a long way in the past ten years, from health and education to science and technology, to communication and transportation. Infant mortality rates have been dramatically declining; in 2000 the rate of infant death was 33 infants per 1000 births dying before age one. It fell to 12 in 2010.[11] Similarly the under-five mortality probability rate dropped from 42 in 2000 to 13 in 2010.[12] Likewise the maternal mortality ratio fell from 36 deaths for every 1000 live births in 2000 to 20 deaths in 2010, while life expectancy increased from an average of 70 in 2000 to 75 in 2009. These developments in healthcare and living standards are, at least in part, the product of policies implemented by the AKP. Government expenditure on health increased from 9.8 percent of the GDP in 2000 to 12.8 percent in 2010. In addition the AKP has spearheaded the Health Transformation Program, a joint project implemented with the World Health Organization in 2003 to improve healthcare services in Turkey. As a result per capita government expenditures on health have increased by 63 percent.[13] What is more, in the past years the party has doled out millions of green cards to the poor, providing for free healthcare to be paid for by the state. In effect, the AKP has re-established Turkey's welfare state that buckled under the population boom in the 1970s.

Education is a similar success story, at least in relative terms. Since 2000 the adult literacy rate has increased by 5 percent and now stands at over 91 percent. Compared to most other Middle Eastern or predominantly Muslim countries, this is an impressive figure. With its high youth literacy (among Turks under fourteen, the literacy rate is already at 98 percent), by the beginning of the next decade Turkey could become the first large Muslim-majority country to attain universal literacy. Turkish higher education stands above its neighbors as well, with eight of the top ten OIC universities housed in Turkey.[14] The country is also promising in research and development; R&D expenditures have increased considerably, from 0.52 percent in 2002 to 0.84 percent in 2009. The number of researchers in research and development per million people has more than doubled, from 366 in 2002 to 803 today, and patent applications among residents have risen dramatically, from 414 in 2002 to 3,885 in 2011.[15]

In the field of communication and transportation Turkey is also taking giant strides, making life easier for common Turks: There were about 7.5 million Internet users in 2002, and there are now 31 million.[16] Similarly, mobile phone subscribers have increased from about 23 million to 65 million. This means that almost 89 percent of the population, a huge majority, owns a mobile phone, whereas in 2002 a mere 36 percent did so. In short, for the average Turk on the street, life has become a bit easier. And these Turks have repaid the AKP at the ballot box.

KEMALISM IS DEAD

Through sound social policies, the AKP has built solid support for its platform, transforming Ataturk's Turkey. Does this suggest that Turkey's twentieth-century experience with Kemalism—a European-oriented, top-down Westernization model—has come to an end? The answer is, to a large extent, yes.

Symbolically speaking, nothing could portend the coming end of Kemalism better than the recent public exoneration of Iskilipli Atif Hoca, a rare resistance figure to Kemalism in the early twentieth century. However, even if Kemalism is withering away, its founder, Ataturk, and his way of doing business seem to be alive in Turkey.

But first the story of Iskilipli Atif Hoca: In November 1925 Ataturk carried out perhaps the most symbolic of his reforms, banning all Turkish males from wearing the Ottoman fez in order to cement his country's commitment to European ideals. Ataturk wanted to make Turks European head to toe, and the abolition of the fez embodied this effort.

Most Turks acquiesced to Ataturk's reforms, not just to the "hat reform" but also to deeper ones such as the "alphabet reform," which changed the Turks' script from an Arab alphabet-based one to its current Latin-based form, further connecting the Turks to European culture. Ataturk was able to achieve these reforms with minor resistance thanks to the weight of his persona. After all, Ataturk—who had just liberated Turkey from a massive Allied occupation—was considered nothing short of a father to all Turks.

Some Turks, however, objected to his reforms. Enter Atif Hoca, a cleric in the small central Anatolian town of Iskilip, not far from Kayseri, who refused to adhere to Ataturk's "hat reform." Atif Hoca defended his use of the fez, couching his objections in Islam. He called for protests against the reforms and began publishing essays in local papers. In February 1926 he was executed by the regime, becoming a rare icon of resistance to Kemalism.

Recently, though, Atif Hoca's legacy has been rehabilitated in the public eye. In February 2012 the AKP government decided to name a public hospital in Iskilip—Atif Hoca's hometown—after him. This dedication carries remarkable symbolic significance; it signals Turkey's move to a post-Kemalist era by honoring one of the best-known anti-Kemalists to date.

ERDOGAN IS NOW MOLDING TURKEY

Even if Turkey has mostly moved beyond Ataturk's legacy in the past decade, an aspect of Ataturk's legacy that seems alive in post-Kemalist Turkey is top-down social engineering. In the same way that Ataturk wanted to shape modern Turkey in his own image, his successors now want to do the same, imposing their own worldview on Turkish society.

In this regard Prime Minister Erdogan is a case in point. Like Ataturk, Erdogan seems willing to use the weight of his personality to remake Turkish society to match his worldview. Erdogan has already led Turkey longer than any other democratically elected prime minister, and he might replace Ataturk as the country's longest-reigning leader if he is elected as the president of Turkey in 2014. Like Ataturk, Erdogan seems willing to use his personal charisma to remake Turkish society to match his vision. Ataturk often said that he wanted "to raise contemporary European generations" among Turks. Recently Erdogan said he "would like to raise religious generations" among the Turks.[17] And Erdogan shows no compunction about meddling in even the most mundane details in the daily lives of citizens, from abortion rights to the type of bread consumed at the dinner table. Prime Minister Erdogan suffered his first major setback in June 2013, when millions of liberal Turks took to the streets to protest the prime minister's impositions on their lifestyles.

BUT "ATATURK" IS ALIVE

Perhaps the most powerful aspect of Ataturk's legacy is that he wanted to restore Turkey's great power status. To this end Ataturk envisaged stripping Turkey of its Ottoman legacy and instilling in it a set of European standards and beliefs so that Turkey could successfully compete against its historic European rivals. In other words, Turkey could become more powerful than Europe only by becoming entirely European itself.

Erdogan and Turkey's new elites have a different view of how to make the country powerful: not by abandoning the country's Ottoman past or by secularizing its religious values, but by embracing them. The ultimate goal, however, remains the same: become powerful enough to compete against the Europeans. Even if the post-Kemalist Turkey is not going to emulate Europe, it will still treat it as a measuring stick.

Ironically, even though Kemalism seems to be out of fashion, its mindset seems nonetheless to have permeated the AKP. In many ways the AKP represents a post-Kemalist Turkey. But eighty years of Kemalism preceding AKP rule, and hundreds of years of Ottoman Westernization before that, have left such an indelible mark on Turkey that even the "post-Kemalist AKP" will follow Ataturk in some ways.

Finally, although the AKP has won its political battle against the secularists, and the party's conservative politics are likely to shape Turkish society in the coming years, there will always be vestiges of Kemalism in this new Turkey that the AKP will need to accommodate.

Surprisingly, though, the list of the vestiges of secular Turkey for which the AKP must make room does not include the secular military, once the most powerful bastion of Kemalism.

3 | The Military Gets on Board

Malatya lies near the Euphrates River in east-central Turkey. It is an Anatolian city of about four hundred thousand inhabitants, and as the base for Turkey's Second Army, it is notable for its large military presence. Malatya is in Turkey's "Koran belt," the country's conservative, Sunni Muslim, and Turkish-dominated heartland that stretches from Afyon in west-central Turkey to Erzurum in the northeast. Malatya stands out with its significant presence of top brass as well as a large cadre of midlevel officers. Throw in the presence of Alevis, who profess a liberal branch of Islam,[1] and it becomes clear how the presence of the secular military in this otherwise conservative Anatolian city serves as a symbol of the role of the military shaping Turkey. Unlike other cities in the "Koran belt," such as Elazig only sixty miles away, Malatya is not suffused with social conservatism. The town has a vibrant social life, including cafes and ice cream parlors frequented by couples on dates, who can be seen promenading on Kanalboyu, a tree-lined boulevard designed during the early days of the Turkish republic. The promenade stretches from the city's Archeological Museum, home of rare Hittite, Roman, and Assyrian antiquities, to the military hotel (*orduevi*), a domineering building that, like others in cities all across Turkey, has come to serve as a symbol of the military's privileged role in Turkish society as well as its watchful position over the country's political system as the guardian of Turkish secularism and Kemalism. Since Turkey witnessed the rise of political Islam in the early 1990s, the Turkish military has increasingly defined itself as the bastion of *laïcité* (European secularism) shaped after the French model of separation of religion and government, providing for a firewall between politics and religion in Turkey. In the last decade, though, the military's symbolic power over Turkish society has eroded. The military's dominant role over Turkish politics has come to an end, the *laïcité* model has collapsed, and the military has become a partner to the Ankara government, fully falling under its power.

THE MILITARY'S SELF-PERCEIVED ROLES

Understanding the Turkish military's historic role as a protector of secularism necessitates a review of Turkey's journey to the West. Contrary to conventional wisdom, the Turkish embrace of the West is not a twentieth-century phenomenon, but rather took place during the Ottoman period after a long period of soul searching with antecedents dating back to the late seventeenth century.

After its massive expansion into Europe the Ottoman Empire suffered a serious military defeat at European hands in Vienna in 1683. Following Vienna, the loss of Hungary and parts of Croatia and Romania to the Austrian Habsburgs ushered in a domino-effect loss of other territories—a series of shocks for the Ottomans.

Until then, the Ottomans had been militarily superior to Western Europeans and had treated them as political inferiors. In 1536, for instance, French king François I wrote to Ottoman sultan Suleyman I, asking for help against the Habsburgs. Suleyman wrote back to François, addressing him as "Francis, king of the province of France,"[2] while introducing himself as

> the sultan of sultans, the sovereign of sovereigns, the dispenser of crowns to the monarchs on the face of the earth, shadow of god on earth, the sultan and sovereign lord of the Mediterranean and the Black Sea, of Rumelia and Anatolia, of Karamania and the land of Rum, of Zulkadria, Diyarbakir, of Kurdistan, of Azerbaijan, Persia, Damascus, Cairo, Aleppo, of the Mecca and Medina, of Jerusalem, of all Arabia, of the Yemen and many other lands,

which my noble forefathers and my glorious ancestors—may God light up their tombs—conquered by the force of their arms and which my august majesty has made subject to my flaming sword and victorious blade, I, Sultan Süleyman Han.[3]

The Ottomans long considered themselves the mighty rulers of the world, but following the Ottoman defeat in Vienna in 1683 and the subsequent loss of territories, the Ottoman elite painfully and gradually conceded to Western superiority. They concluded that the only way to defeat Europe was to become European. Because the most obvious sign of Ottoman weakness compared to Europe was in the military realm, the empire decided to create a European military.

Accordingly, following the Russian example and heralding the subsequent case of Japanese modernization, the Ottoman dynasty moved ahead with military westernization to match Europe. In 1773 the sultan set up a modern, Western military school, the Imperial School of Naval Engineering (*Muhendishane-i Bahri-i Humayun*), to create a Western navy, the military backbone of all European powers at the time. This school provided a secular, science-based, and European curriculum. What is more, many of its instructors were of Western European origin. Gradually, similar schools followed, all with Western and secular curricula (see photo). A new cadre of Western-minded officers was trained in these schools, forming the "New Army" (*Nizam-i Cedid*), which supplanted the rank and file of the traditional Ottoman army, the Janissary Corps (*Yeniceriler*). The experiment proved successful; by the early nineteenth century the New Army had 22,700 soldiers and 1,600 officers.[4] This process was completed in 1826 by Sultan Mahmud II with the abolition of the janissary order, the traditional core of the Ottoman military, and its substitution by a solidly Western Ottoman army that had increasingly secular-minded and Western-trained officers.[5]

The Kuleli Military High School in Istanbul, established in 1845, is one of several Ottoman military schools established to provide secular Western curricula. Housed in a building with visible elements of European architecture, Kuleli also symbolizes Ottoman military Westernization efforts.

Fig. 1. Kuleli Military High School.
Courtesy of José Luiz Bernardes Ribeiro / CC-BY-SA-3.0.

With its Westernization experience solidly beginning in 1773, the Turkish military's memory of being Western predates France's memory of being a republic. The Turkish military, thoroughly secularized under Ataturk, remained committed to being Western and secular. However, as Turkey modernized and progressed, this stance failed to keep pace as the military held fast to notions of Westernization and secularism that were in vogue during the early part of the twentieth century. Unable to renew its ideological stance, the military was ripe for challenge from Turkey's fast-changing society. In the end it would be the AKP that would truly take them to task.

It is no coincidence that Ataturk, the leading figure of Westernization in modern Turkey, arose from the Ottoman army. At the end of World War I Ataturk not only liberated Turkey, but also established a fully European republic that recognized only secular laws and provided only secular education.

On April 10, 1928, the Turkish parliament eliminated from the constitution the declaration of Islam as Turkey's state religion.[6] European style secularism, or *laïcité*, was an important part of Ataturk's secular vision. As Ataturk pushed to Westernize Turkey, he looked to France for ideas. Ataturk's foreign language was French, and like most educated people of his time, he grew up with exposure to the intellectual milieu of nineteenth-century French intellectuals and sociologists, such as positivists Emile Durkheim and Auguste Comte. These ideas of linear historical progress might have influenced young Mustafa Kemal. Moreover, as in many other countries, in Turkey the lodestar for political reform and Westernization was France in the nineteenth and early twentieth centuries. Hence, both the Ottoman Empire and Ataturk's Turkey established many institutions in accordance with the French model. Like France, Turkey became a highly centralized country, with a strong national identity. The similarity is also manifest in the way the two countries practice secularism. Unlike American secularism, which has historically provided "freedom *of* religion" for people fleeing religious persecution, European (French and Turkish) secularism (*laïcité*) was born in reaction to the domination of the political sphere by one faith. It has thus promoted "freedom *from* religion." As it matured under Ataturk in Turkey, therefore, *laïcité* defined Islam as a private matter to be relegated to the private sphere. With this framework, *laïcité* set up a state-controlled firewall between religion and politics, thicker than that of American secularism, banning what is considered religious symbols, such as the Islamic-style headscarf, in politics. This firewall later became the biggest challenge to Islamist politicians in Turkey, as well their most determined target. The Turks also put their own twist on the *laïcité* model by codifying state-control over religious institutions. This seemed like a natural course of action for the Turkish Republic, given that during the Ottoman era the Sultan was empowered to dismiss, and even execute, the highest Muslim clergyman at his pleasure.

Ataturk's vision was that the military, as modern Turkey's most Western institution, would guard his legacy, including secularism, though he never gave the military such a task. The military legally self-assigned the task of preserving Turkey's secular constitution after carrying out the republic's first coup against the center-right and conservative DP government of Adnan Menderes. Article 35 of the Internal Service Law of the military, put in place after the 1960 coup d'état, stipulated that the Turkish Armed Forces were responsible for "guarding and defending the Turkish Republic as defined by the constitution." The military has acted on this self-appointed legal obligation, acting successfully to oust the Welfare Party government in 1997, but failing to do so against the AKP in 2007.

Regardless of their legal authority, what explains the Turkish military's comfort in past interventions in politics? Turkish opinion polls have consistently showed the military as the most respected institution in the country. A 2002 poll by the Washington DC–based Pew Center showed that the military is the institution most liked by the Turks, more than the government, the parliament, the media, and the mosque. Some 79 percent said that the military was a good influence in the country, whereas the approval rate was 7 percent for the prime minister, 7 percent for the national government, 32 percent for religious leaders, and 47 percent for the media.[7]

From where do the military derive their popularity? First, the fact that the military under Ataturk liberated Turkey against what appeared to be impossible odds has ensured that Turks across the political spectrum, including the Islamists, recognize them as a national savior. A second contributing factor is that they conscript across all of Turkey's social classes, ethnic groups, and regions. Acting as a social leveler and a democratizing institution, the military provides a rare chance for upward mobility. Third, many Turks respect the military because, unlike the political classes, their reputations have not been dragged through the mud amid charges of corruption and malfeasance, until recently, that is.

POPULAR VIEWS ON THE TURKISH MILITARY

Popular trust in the military has, however, had the side effect of producing a sort of "political atrophy" among the secularists. Secular parties and the population at large often turn to the military for "political housecleaning," as they did during the "February 28th Process" in the late 1990s when the military acted to force out a government coalition that included the Islamist Welfare Party. In this episode Turkey's secularists prodded the military to take action, rather than playing fair in the game of politics. Indeed, for much of Turkey's history, the middle classes especially have taken comfort in the military as a secular firewall against Islamism.

Despite the military's popularity, the Turks have developed a cynical attitude to military-backed candidates. Although the people supported the military's role in political housecleaning, they shy away from voting for parties that appear to be the military's candidates. In the aftermath of Turkey's last coup in 1980, for instance, the military-backed Nationalist Democracy Party, led by a retired general, came in last in the elections. The party least favored by the military, Turgut Ozal's ANAP, emerged victorious. This shows the Turkish public's political bias against candidates favored by the military and toward those considered the underdog to the military. This perception also helped the AKP win against the military in the 2007 elections that centered on disagreement with the military concerning Abdullah Gul's bid for the Turkish presidency. Although the Welfare Party had failed to stand up to the military and challenge Turkish secularism, the AKP succeeded by standing up to the military while maintaining public support. Erdogan's pluck against the military has contributed to his stature and helped build his image as a tough guy and a likeable underdog.

FAREWELL TO THE ARMY

In addition to the AKP's electoral success, other factors also led to the demise of the Turkish military's dominant role over politics. Until only a few years ago military officers from the rank of general to lieutenant would not flinch in criticizing Turkey's civilian leaders and voicing—sometimes even imposing—their views on Turkey's politicians. The AKP has changed all of this with a strategy that consisted of two decisive moves. First, they launched Turkey on a path of economic growth, building a significant and broad base to support their agenda. Then, backed by their coalition of poor voters and Anatolian Tigers, they instituted sweeping institutional reforms that dismantled many of the military's former advantages. These reforms not only served to qualify

Turkey for EU accession, but they also eliminated the military's role in civilian politics. This sweep culminated in the controversial Ergenekon case that has imprisoned a sizable portion of Turkey's top-level military brass under suspicion of coup plotting and has broken the military's back. During the summer of 2012 more than 30 percent of Turkey's generals and admirals were facing criminal charges, with half of those charged sitting behind bars without chance of bail.

In the past decade the military has played its hand badly, making missteps that have allowed the AKP to subjugate the armed forces to its power. The Turkish military shied away from issuing an opinion on the Iraq War in 2003, surprising many analysts who were accustomed to the military calling the shots on key foreign policy issues in Ankara. In doing this the military hoped to put the onus of a tough and potentially risky war decision on the AKP. In the end the AKP had its cake and ate it too. The governing party agreed to work with Washington in Iraq, but then a parliamentary motion needed to authorize Turkey's participation in the war failed in the Turkish parliament on technical grounds—the motion that was supported by a majority of the representatives in the Turkish legislative failed to pass for not getting the backing of the necessary quorum. Turkey did not enter the war, and the AKP was spared the political repercussions of a risky decision, and yet this was the first time the military had not called the shots on a major foreign policy issue. This was the beginning of the end of the military's role in Turkish politics: the Turkish military started to lose the power that it did not exercise.

The Turkish military belatedly stood up to the AKP in 2007, issuing a declaration on its website in which it warned the governing party, saying "radical Islamic understanding . . . has been expanding its sphere with encouragement from politicians and local authorities." The statement added: "the Turkish Armed Forces . . . are staunch defenders of secularism . . . and will display their position and attitudes when it becomes necessary."[8]

In the past when the military stood up to civilian government, politicians would listen to the generals. This was the case for Necmettin Erbakan, head of the Islamist Welfare Party during the 1990s. At the time when the military issued a memorandum, also known as the "February 28 process" against Erbakan's Welfare Party's participation in a coalition government, Erbakan simply conceded defeat and resigned on June 18, 1997.

This did not happen in 2007. When the military issued its memorandum on April 28, 2007, the AKP did not flinch. Instead, Cemil Cicek, at the time deputy prime minister with the AKP, said: "The General Staff's adoption of any such position against the government is unacceptable in a state operating under the rule of law."[9] What is more, Gul announced that he would not back down from his candidacy. The military was dumbstruck by this unexpected civilian defiance and suddenly found itself in an impossible dilemma: either stage a coup or stay quiet. Not wanting to engage in a takeover that could result in economic meltdown and a potential mess on its hands, the military stayed quiet, and the AKP won. For the second time in five years the military's prestige eroded because the institution called into question the power everyone believed it had. The military proved itself an empty shell, unable to back its words with acts. The military's 2003 and 2007 missteps damaged the way the Turks perceived it: the Turkish military finally came down to earth. But for an already defeated Turkish military, it took the Ergenekon case to break its back.

ENTER ERGENEKON

In 2007 Turkish law enforcement began a sweep of arrests against military and civilians on suspicion of conspiring to orchestrate a coup d'état against Turkey's elected leaders. And so began the Ergenekon saga. With the Ergenekon case, the AKP has embarked on simultaneous persecution and prosecution of the opposition—both in the military and in the civilian realm. For the last several decades the Turkish military was untouchable; no one dared to criticize the military or its top generals, lest they risk getting burned. The Turkish Armed Forces were the ultimate protectors of founding father Mustafa Kemal Ataturk's secular legacy, and no other force in the country could seriously threaten its supremacy. Not anymore.

Since 2007 hundreds of people have been arrested, including Army officers, but also opponents of the government, renowned journalists, university presidents, artists, and women's rights activists, as well as radical right-wing activists and retired generals with links to the criminal underworld, all collectively charged with plotting to overthrow the government.

Instead of prosecuting criminals, who seem to have been involved in discussing, though probably not executing, a coup against the government, the government has used this fluid case to persecute its opponents. Since 2007 the police have taken more than five hundred people into custody, sometimes without evidence of criminal activity, only to release many of them without charge after a few days of harsh questioning. Following their release, most become docile intellectuals. Meanwhile, police have held some AKP opponents for years without charge—a strong signal to Turkey's intellectuals of the cost of not supporting the AKP.

The AKP's attempts to subjugate the media have taken other forms as well. The national police, controlled by the government, wiretap journalists and politicians on the grounds that they are connected to Ergenekon. Wiretaps are another tool for harassing liberal and secular Turks. On April 26, 2009, Turkey's justice minister said that police intelligence listens to the private conversations of seventy thousand people; almost one in every thousand Turks lives under police scrutiny today.

In Turkey it is illegal to wiretap private conversations without a court order or publish conversations captured by the police. However, pro-AKP media outlets regularly published wiretapped conversations of the AKP's opponents, compromising their private lives and even alleging that they are "terrorists" connected to Ergenekon. The AKP does not prosecute these crimes, which have the effect of terrorizing liberal intellectuals.

To some, it might appear that the newfound freedom to criticize the military proves that Turkey is becoming a more liberal democracy. But the truth is that Turkey has replaced one "untouchable" organization for another. Illegal wiretaps and arbitrary arrests serve to intimidate the public, not prosecute criminals.

Hundreds of arrests later, the case has yet to reach a complete and final verdict. Yet, the Turkish military has borne the brunt of these arrests. Around half of all Turkish naval admirals have been jailed at one point or another.

Moreover, because all of the air force's four-star generals have been implicated, it was not certain that Turkey's military promotions board would even have a four-star general to promote to Chief of Air Force during its annual meeting in August 2011. Consequently in 2011 the joke in Ankara had become, "Thank God Greece is in an economic meltdown; otherwise this would be the perfect time to invade Turkey!"

And then the military snapped. The straw that broke the camel's back came when pro-government media suggested that fourteen active-duty generals and admirals who had been arrested in relationship to the Ergenekon case, though not yet indicted, would not only be bypassed in their promotions but would also be forced to resign in summer 2011.[10] The police then arrested twenty-two additional top brass officers, blocking their likely promotions. For the first time in its life, the Turkish military was caught like a deer in headlights, facing the political high beams of the Ergenekon case.

THE MILITARY'S DIMINISHING POPULARITY

Historically the most respected institution in the country and the king-maker in Ankara, the military has seen its prestige and power free fall since the AKP took power in 2002. Coup allegations, including assertions that the military was planning to bomb Istanbul's historic mosques to precipitate a political crisis, have hurt the Turkish army's standing. The military's status as the most trusted institution in the country is plummeting: in 2002 around 79 percent of the Turks said they trusted their military, while recent polls show that barely 66 percent say they do.[11] What is more, with dozens of generals and hundreds of other officers in jail for years for coup allegations, with no indictment in sight, the officer corps is demoralized. When the military's top brass resigned en masse in summer 2011, they in effect breathed their last gasps of political relevance. "We are done fighting, you win," was the message that emerged from the episode. In other words the military agreed to work with and under the AKP.

The Turkish military lost its battle against the AKP primarily because it lost its virtual power over Turkish society. All this has not been without consequences. Applications and graduation numbers for army high schools, once considered prestigious institutions, have dramatically dropped from 66,000 and 895, respectively, in 2007 to 45,000 and 305, respectively, in 2011.

The military now comes under daily attacks for its failures and perceived failures. Take, for instance, a 2012 case in Semdinli, a border town in southeast Turkey where the military launched a ten-day operation after an opposition parliamentarian claimed that the zone was in fact under the control of the PKK, and that the Turkish Armed Forces had no authority in that region. These claims were rejected by various people in the government, including the prime minister; this surprising development suggests that Erdogan considers the military his own, rising to its defense. Nevertheless the events have planted a seed of doubt about the military's ability to hold its monopoly of force over Turkey's territory.

Other examples where the military came under unprecedented public scrutiny include a September 2012 explosion at Afyon in which twenty-five soldiers died as a result of what seemed to be an accidental explosion in an ammunition depot. However, Kemal Kilicdaroglu, the leader of the main opposition CHP, alleged that the explosion was the result of sabotage, suggesting military incompetence,[12] a shocking and yet telling development about the military's lingering relationship to the Kemalist legacy given that the CHP, Ataturk's party, would have until recently shied away from criticizing the military. Military prosecutors said that no evidence of sabotage had been found, while four commanders were removed from their positions after the deadly incident.

Last but not least, recently the Turkish military suffered a blow on the international stage when a Turkish fighter jet was shot down by the Syrian military in June 2012. Given the fact that its perceived power has all but evaporated, the military now comes under criticism for failing to defeat the PKK. It has been accused of being inefficient, unaccountable, and careless in its operations and dealings with the PKK. In 2010 the conservative *Zaman* newspaper encapsulated this sentiment when it opined that "with its current mindset, personnel, and structure, the military, quite frankly, cannot defeat the PKK."[13]

THE AKP'S MILITARY?

Losing its popularity, the Turkish military will increasingly look for shelter under the wings of the governing party. This new alignment is most apparent in Turkey's response to the Syrian uprising, as well as in the country's policies against the PKK. The risk of the civil war next door in Syria spilling into Turkey has tightened the relationship that emerged between the AKP and the military in 2011, with the military agreeing to work under the AKP. This common front was displayed during the Turkish military response to Assad's artillery barrages across the Syrian border into Turkish towns. The Turkish military's chief-of-staff Necdet Ozel's reaction to these barrages was completely in line with the government's policy objectives. And when General Ozel's tactics came under criticism in the media, Turkey's deputy prime minister Bulent Arinc came to Ozel's defense, showing that the AKP is confident in its 'ownership' of the military.[14]

For the past decade a military versus AKP dichotomy has shaped most analysis on Turkey. A new relationship now seems to be emerging. Policy differences between the AKP and the military leadership are melting away, with the two joining around a nationalist foreign policy line. In this regard the governing party and the military will likely coalesce around the AKP's foreign policy doctrine, containing a nativist streak that the AKP has implemented to make the country a regional power. Accordingly there will be close cooperation between the government and the military on key foreign policy issues, ranging from Cyprus to ties with Israel and to handling the crisis in Syria.

With the AKP abandoning its erstwhile conciliatory attitude on the issue of the divided island of Cyprus, the party will increasingly confront the Greek Cypriots on oil and gas exploration and drilling projects in the Eastern Mediterranean. Whereas Greek Cypriots are proceeding with plans to issue licenses to international companies for oil or gas exploration in the Eastern Mediterranean, Turkey is running interference with a mix of military threats and legal challenges. Turkish foreign minister Ahmet Davutoglu warned the Greek Cypriots in August 2011 that if exploratory drilling goes ahead, Turkey would react with the "necessary response" against such an action.

A combative tone on the Cyprus issue resonates well with the military, but it is ultimately harmful to Turkey's credibility in Western circles. As Turkey's EU negotiations show signs of revival in the coming year, Turkey's leaders may look to soften this tone.

Yet on a variety of other foreign policy issues, the AKP is likely to take the lead with a nationalist stance, with the military following in step. For example, Turkey's policy on Syria has been determined by the AKP, with the military helping in the execution of this policy. Warming ties with Israel could also create a space for the military to play a role, if the two countries decide to restore their longstanding military-to-military ties.

Since 2002 Turkey has been at a turning point in terms of its politics. Bolstered by economic growth and a gradual, if zigzagging, ascent to regional power status, the AKP has emerged as the country's dominant political force. With the unceremonious removal of the military, once considered a political check and balance, the AKP's preponderance in Turkish politics may have reached its zenith.

4 | Is Turkish Power Myth or Reality?

With the rise of Erdogan and the AKP, Turkey has set its sights on becoming a regional power, projecting its influence across its neighborhood and even globally. This global political vision is best observed in the Turkish capital, Ankara, a lone city that sits in the middle of a vast plateau. Ankara is flanked by the Anatolian Steppe to the south and the west and the Elmadagi and Huseyin Gazi Mountains to the east and the north. The two grey peaks and the steppe that encircle the city give it a sense of isolation from the rest of the world, especially during the cold winter months when snow covers the Anatolian interior. Ataturk is said to have picked Ankara as his capital for its location in the middle of Anatolia, which kept it safe from potential Allied occupation. He also favored it for its access to a trunk railway line from Istanbul, which kept Ataturk connected to the world.

In the past decade, Ankara, as the seat of Turkish foreign policy, has embodied Turkey's new foreign policy. Previously, over the course of the twentieth century, Turkey's world had become increasingly Eurocentric. The country joined Western institutions, such as the OECD in 1960 and moved to become a member to the EU, applying for union membership in 1959 and 1987 but beginning official negotiations only in 2005.

AWAY FROM EUROPE

Today, however, the country's single-minded European trajectory appears to be a thing of the past. Turkey has experienced phenomenal

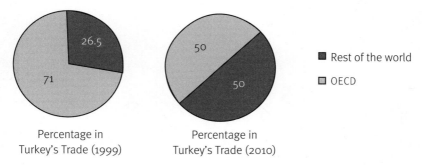

TABLE 1. Turkey's Changing World

Percentage in
Turkey's Trade (1999)

Percentage in
Turkey's Trade (2010)

■ Rest of the world
☐ OECD

economic growth in the past decade and is no longer content to subsume itself under Europe. Since 2002 the Turkish economy has nearly trebled in size, reaching a magnitude of $1.3 trillion. Gone is the Turkey of yesteryear, a poor country begging to get into the EU, and in its place is a new Turkey, confident and booming as the world around it suffers from economic meltdown. Europe's economic doldrums coupled with Turkey's new trans-European vision under the AKP government mean that the country's traditional commercial bonds with Europe are eroding while its trade links with the non-European world flourish. Accordingly the Turks are increasingly trading with the non-OECD world. In parallel with this trend, Ankara has pursued a foreign policy that transcends Turkey's old European focus.

LIKED BY THE ARABS

To this end the Turks have reached far and wide to build soft power, the ability to get things done without use of force. Recently the Syrian uprising has represented a challenge to that goal in regions Turkey had earlier ignored, such as the Middle East, Africa, and far-flung countries such as Vietnam and Mongolia. Ankara's quest for power is driven by economic dynamism, political stability, and a new supra-European vision. The private sector, universities, and NGOs are driving this agenda, shaping the new Turkish supra-European identity. Will the Turkish quest for soft power succeed? Will Turkey achieve its goal to

TABLE 2. Number of New Diplomatic Missions, 1999–2011

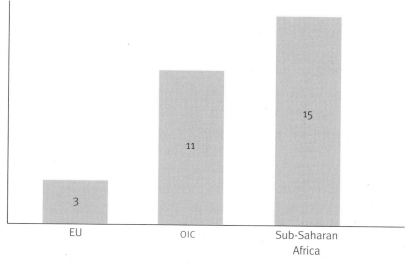

Source: Turkish Republic Ministry of Foreign Affairs official website (http://www.mfa.gov.tr).

become a country that is liked, emulated, and followed by the Middle East and North Africa, and even countries further afield?

The artifacts of Turkey's new soft power can be found across the Middle East, from Turkish products that fill store shelves to the massive success of Turkish soap operas and films. Today forty-two Turkish television dramas are on air in the Arab world. The first program to hit the Arabic airwaves, *Silver*, broke ratings records with 85 million viewers in Arab countries.

Turkey's desire to project its power around the world is most tangibly visible in the Turkish foreign ministry. As telling as buildings can be of the institutions they host, the foreign ministry's main building in Ankara's Balgat district was, until recently an inside-out concrete, brutalist high-rise. Recently, however, the Turkish foreign ministry publicized its plans to build a vast, state-of-the-art, light-filled, and landscaped horizontal campus to house the country's growing cadre of diplomats. This is fitting of the foreign ministry's grandiose vision for Turkey's future.

Another political indicator of Turkey's vision of reaching beyond Europe is a breakdown of the number of new diplomatic missions Turkey has opened up since the AKP came to power in 2002.

The preponderance of new Turkish missions in non-European countries demonstrates that Ankara's foreign policy vision aims to reach beyond Europe. Animated by Foreign Minister Davutoglu's vision of "strategic depth," in the past decade, this vision has moved Turkish diplomats to build clout for Turkey in the Middle East, Africa, and Muslim-majority countries. In the past decade the foreign ministry has opened four new diplomatic missions in the developed OECD countries, while its real outreach has been toward the emerging countries of the global south. Turkey has opened eleven new missions in states that are members of the OIC and expanded its diplomatic representation in the Middle East, opening three new consulates in Iraq, for example, since 2007. Yet the most drastic expansion has been in Africa, where Turkey has tripled its missions, opening fifteen embassies in 2010–2011 alone, including missions in Abuja and Banjul. Drawn by a spirit of political and economic adventure, Ankara has plunged enthusiastically into Africa. The AKP dubbed 2005 "The Year of Africa," and Erdogan made the first visit to sub-Saharan Africa of any Turkish prime minister, landing Turkey an observer seat in the African Union. Currently Turkish peacekeepers are active in five African nations, and the Turkish navy takes part in anti-piracy operations off the Horn of Africa.[1] But Turkey's engagement in Africa is more than just an idealistic endeavor; Turkey sees great commercial potential in Africa's long-impoverished national economies, and the Turks have made themselves a reputation in Africa for inexpensive, high-quality exports.

Turkey's leaders are leveraging this soft power, forming ties with international civil society and establishing a presence in an array of international forums. To this end Ankara's ambition knows almost no limits. Turkey has established observer status at the Arab League and participates in nearly every conference. In 2005 the OIC appointed a Turk, Ekmeleddin Ihsanoglu, as general secretary. Turkey was selected as an IMF executive director for 2014, and Turkey is slated to host the G20 summit in 2015. Turkey has also put itself in the running for the 2020 Olympic Games, the 2020 World Expo, and a seat in the UN Security Council in 2015. It is even participating in more far-flung forums, such as the Asia-Pacific Economic Cooperation organization and Association of Caribbean States.

At the same time, Ankara is firmly holding onto its long-standing membership in classic and powerful Western institutions, such as the OECD, Council of Europe, and NATO, as well as in non–Middle Eastern and non-Muslim regional institutions, such as the Black Sea Forum. But Turkish diplomats are dreaming beyond the regional stage. Turkey is looking for a seat at every table and a membership card in every club. To this end Ankara has even sought a place at the table with the quirky "Developing 8," a forum for developing economies that includes Bangladesh, Egypt, Indonesia, Iran, Malaysia, Nigeria, and Pakistan. Turkey also observes at organizations that focus on issues in the Western Hemisphere, such as the Association of Caribbean States and Organization of American States. Turkey's foreign policy elites are convinced that Turkey's role in shaping world affairs extends beyond its local geography. Foreign Minister Davutoglu summarized this ambition best when he proclaimed, "This is a new global order in the making, and Turkey is doing its best to contribute to the successful completion of this transition period."

To some extent, this energetic outreach is limited by shortages in Turkey's concrete capacities. The soft power that Ankara wishes to gain through diplomatic representation may face material constraints. For example, as of June 2012 Turkey's Foreign Ministry had only about 135 career staff posted in the Middle East in over twenty-five missions. Moreover, only 6 of these diplomats appeared to be fluent in Arabic. What is more, despite its global ambitions, the foreign ministry staffs only 5,533 personnel, a measly number compared to Germany's 12,437 foreign affairs employees or the UK's 17,100. These shortages expose the gap between Turkey's aspirations and actual capacity, requiring Turkey to find creative ways to punch above its weight in many arenas. In the past years the foreign ministry has started to hire more people, increasing its quota for newly hired diplomats from just around 20 in 2005 to over 100 in 2012.

Turkey's involvement in Somalia is a prime illustration of this tendency to dream big, even if Turkish abilities remain modest. For the past several years Turkish leaders have made a splash by pushing to involve themselves in Somalia's political fate and economic development. As famine devastated the country in 2011, Prime Minister Erdogan traveled to Mogadishu to express his solidarity with the Somalis. Calls to aid the Somalis hit the airwaves and newspapers across Turkey, and the Turkish public responded by raising over $60 million for Somalia. Turkey's Foreign Minister Davutoglu called on the world to "do their part not only for short-term humanitarian assistance but the long-term economic development of Somalia," pledging that Turkey would "continue to work for our brothers and sisters [in Somalia] and we will never leave them alone."[2]

But Turkey's actual presence on the ground is much smaller than this rhetoric might suggest. For instance, most of Turkey's development work is handled by NGOs with tiny staffs. The largest NGO, Turkey's Red Crescent (Kizilay) had only ten Turkish personnel in Mogadishu in May 2012. The Turkish government has been working to coordinate aid on the ground by sending the Turkish Cooperation and Coordination Agency (TIKA), its own version of USAID, to the scene, but in June 2012 it only had a single Turkish staff member on the ground in Mogadishu. Yet regardless of the odds, Turkey's leaders maintain they are steadfast in their commitment to the country. This combination of earnest ambition and limited means has become a hallmark of Turkey's recent engagements around the world.

THE COUNTRY EVERYONE WANTS TO VISIT

It will be a while before Ankara's diplomatic means match its ambitions. In the meantime the bulk of Turkey's soft power is likely to emanate from more informal sources, including a global network of schools run by the Gulen Movement. Consider tourism, for instance. Over the past decade, the number of tourists traveling to Turkey has tripled; Turkey is now the sixth most visited country, and Istanbul is the tenth most visited city in the world.[3]

This is a matter of built capacity, a factor of the country's economic growth: in 2011, some 117 million international travelers went through Turkish airports, and Turkey's hotel industry can accommodate over 1 million visitors at one time.[4]

Europeans make up the lion's share of these visitors, but Turkey has become a major tourist destination for its Middle Eastern neighbors as well. While a decade ago, only 7 percent of Turkey's tourists were from the Middle East, today over 12 percent come from the region, adding up to over 3 million Middle Eastern tourists per year. This figure includes 175,000 visitors from Saudi Arabia, 48,000 from the UAE, 533,000 from Iraq, and 144,000 from Lebanon in 2012.[5] In fact, this increase in Middle East tourists seems to be a consequence to the Arab Spring and the fall of several dictatorships across the region. For example, in 2010 only 60,917 Libyans visited Turkey. In 2012, following Qadhafi's fall, this number jumped to 213,890.[6]

In addition to a sharp increase in Arab tourists, Turkey is already the choice destination for Iranians, who are the third largest nationality among visitors to Turkey. In 2011, 1.8 million Iranians vacationed in Turkish resorts, most of them beach vacations, an elusive form of relaxation in Iran. Arabs and Iranians alike are choosing Turkey for its modern amenities and open mindset when it comes to tourism. For many visitors from the Arab world, Turkey is the perfect mix of the familiar and the novel. As a Kuwaiti visitor describes it, "It is a comfortable country from an Islamic point of view, and at the same time, its atmosphere is more European."[7]

THE FIRST UNIVERSALLY LITERATE LARGE MUSLIM SOCIETY

Turkey's desire to build soft power in Muslim-majority countries also resides in the fact that it is potentially the best educated large Muslim society. Illiteracy is nearing extinction in Turkey. In 1990 the adult literacy rate was only 79 percent. Today over 91 percent of Turks can read and write, and 98 percent of young people are literate, suggesting that Turkey is set to become the first large Muslim society with universal literacy within a generation.[8]

The Turks are getting better educated overall. More students are partaking in secondary school studies than ever before, with an enrollment rate of 67 percent, up from 37 percent just a decade ago. To accommodate this wave of new students, the number of universities in Turkey rose from 74 to 166 over the past decade, with public institutions offering quality instruction and low tuition rates.

TURKEY AND THE ARAB SPRING

A third source of Turkey's soft power lies in the country's newfound role in the Arab Spring. Even before the Arab Spring, Ankara had already built influence in the Middle East and North Africa by fostering business networks and establishing state-of-the-art high schools to educate the future Arab elite. A recent survey by the Turkish Economic and Social Studies Foundation (TESEV), an Istanbul-based think tank, measured perceptions of Turkey in the Middle East. According to the poll, Turkey is the most popular country in the region. Over 90 percent of Libyans and Tunisians view Turkey favorably, with Palestinians and Saudis not far behind with 89 percent. Across the Middle East, those polled responded favorably to questions about Turkey's role in the region. When asked if Turkey should play a bigger role in the Middle East, 71 percent of respondents in the region said yes, and 61 percent of those polled thought Turkey could serve as a model for their own country.[9]

Following the Arab Spring, Turkey has even more clout in the region: "Most people in the Middle East view Turkey's accomplishments as being replicable," said Khairi Abaza, an expert on Arab politics based in Washington DC. "Turkey was once like us, and that is why we like it, for it suggests a way forward."

These are the lasting ingredients of Turkish soft power. Turkish products dominate shops across the region, and Turkish soap operas depict educated and emancipated women against the background of a modern and functioning society. Turkey seems to offer an appealing, attainable social model, and the Arab Spring is providing Turkey with an opportunity to spread its influence even farther.

In the past decade Ankara has followed the political route toward cultivating its soft power. The Turkish government has shown its solidarity with Muslim causes in the region, building a rapport with Arab governments in ways unimaginable during the era of westward-looking Kemalism in Turkey.

At first this meant distancing Turkish foreign policy from the United States. Yet amid the squalls of the Arab Spring, Ankara has come to realize the value of its strong ties with the West. If it wants to keep its influence in Arab countries, Turkey needs to prove it is more than a "wealthy Yemen," that is, a prosperous, large Muslim nation with no real value added to regional security.

Ultimately Turkey has come to understand that its strategic value to the Middle East is not rooted in the fact that it is a Muslim power—the region has many such states—but that it is a Muslim power with strong ties to the United States and access to NATO resources. This realization was the catalyst for Ankara's foreign policy turnaround. One example of this was Turkey's strategic decision to join NATO's missile defense project in September 2011.

Similarly, Arabs care less that Turkey is a Muslim country than that it is a democracy. According to the recent Arab public opinion poll conducted by the Brookings Institute, Turkey is the biggest winner of the Arab Spring and was chosen by Arabs as the country that has played the "most constructive" role in the region. When asked this question, twice as many Arabs voted for Turkey than voted for the United States.[10]

Still, challenges remain for Turkey's potential role in the Arab Spring. First, Turkey faces the temptations of "Ottomania," idealizing the past to the extent that the Turks sometimes fail to see that not everyone remembers the Ottomans fondly. Emboldened by record-breaking economic growth over the past decade, the Turks are, once again, feeling imperial. And neo-Ottomanism is becoming the political lens through which many Turks view world politics. Indeed, the Turks' benign view of Ottoman rule in the Middle East hardly resembles what the Arabs remember. For the Arabs the Ottomans were cruel masters, and no one wants them to return as modern big brothers. In 2007 when I visited Damascus, my guide chose to start my tour with the Marjeh Square. "This is where your grandparents executed mine," said my otherwise affable guide, referring to the May 6, 1916, "Martyrs' Day" execution of Arab nationalist leaders, including the journalist Abdelhamid al-Zahrawi and the poet Rafik Salloum, at the hands of the Ottoman Turks. If the Arabs start to see Turkey as a neo-Ottomanist entity, Ankara could encounter pushback as it tries to lead political developments in the region.

Turkey's latest challenge will be proving its credentials as a liberal democracy. As debate continues on drafting its first civilian-made constitution, this is an especially important point. In this regard, Ankara's recent decision to start Kurdish-language classes in public schools is a step in the right direction. This move could help alleviate the Kurdish problem in the country and provide more diversity within Turkey. In order for Turkey to rise as a regional power and lead the movement for democratic change, it must first win the battle for liberal democracy at home.

Even if it were to become a more likeable player across the Middle East and North Africa, Turkey may find it difficult to turn this perception into actual power by becoming a country that is seen as a model. Turkey's experience in the past decade under the AKP government—blending democracy, close ties with the West, a "Muslim" foreign policy, capitalism, and Islamism—may not be so easily copied by Arab societies.

TURKEY'S DOUBLE PIVOT: AWAY FROM WASHINGTON AND THEN CLOSER

Although rooted in Turkey's unabashedly antidemocracy Islamist movement, the AKP became more moderate, declaring its commitment to democracy, before it came to power in 2002. And once in power, the party pursued a policy that delivered phenomenal economic growth. It thereby became so popular that it was able to reshape Turkey, bringing the once-dominant military under its control and the elites into its camp.

Meanwhile the AKP has done a near full circle in foreign policy. Initially the party confronted the United States on key issues, including the Iraq War, Israel, and Iran's nuclear program, in the hope of casting Turkey as a "Muslim power." This pivot away from the West nearly spoiled Turkey's unique identity. The nation entered a period of increasingly cold relations with the United States and turned its interest to the Middle East in hopes of becoming a regional power.

But lately, the party has shifted, moving closer to U.S. positions on Iran and also cooperating with Washington in Libya and then Syria. Ankara also refused to allow a "second flotilla" to sail to Israel from Turkish waters in June 2011, a move promoted by Washington that helped prevent further Turkish-Israeli conflict. Turkey and Israel were able to make amends and re-establish diplomatic contact. Finally, during a visit to Cairo in 2011 Erdogan made a ringing appeal for secularism as an important component of democracy, saying, "I recommend a secular constitution for Egypt. Do not fear secularism because it does not mean being an enemy of religion. I hope the new regime in Egypt will be secular. I hope that after these remarks of mine the way the Egyptian people look at secularism will change."[11]

A major driver of Turkey's foreign policy pivot has been the Arab Spring, which has led Ankara again to embrace its old friends in Washington. The Arab Spring has exposed the limits of Turkey's "act alone" strategy in the Middle East. In particular the uprising in Syria has demonstrated that Turkey cannot deal with massive regional instability unilaterally. Ankara asked for NATO assistance to contain the fallout of the Syria crisis in late 2011 and deal with refugee flows from Syria, as well as requesting German and Dutch Patriot air defense missiles for deployment along the border with Syria.

When the Syrian uprising began in the spring of 2011, Turkish leaders initially encouraged Bashar al-Assad's regime to reform. In August 2011 Davutoglu spent six hours in Damascus asking Assad to stop killing civilians.[12]

Damascus not only disregarded Turkey's pleas; it sent tanks into Hama within hours of Davutoglu's departure from the Syrian capital. Following this affront Ankara broke from Assad and began calling for his ouster. Turkey began providing safe haven to Syrian opposition groups, and media reports have even indicated that Ankara has been arming the Syrian rebels.[13]

Assad responded by letting the PKK operate in Syria after keeping a lid on the group for more than a decade. In 1998 Assad's father had cracked down on the longtime presence of Kurdish militants in Syria, after Turkey threatened to invade if Syria continued to harbor the PKK. In spring 2011 Assad allowed the PKK to move some two thousand militants into Syria from their mountain enclave in northern Iraq,[14] in effect signaling to Ankara: "Help my enemy, and I will help yours."

Tehran has spoken in similar tones. In September 2011, immediately after Ankara started to confront the Assad regime, Tehran reconciled with the PKK's Iranian franchise, the PJAK. Tehran had been fighting its Kurdish rebels since 2003 as part of a strategy to take advantage of the rift between Turkey and the United States at the onset of the Iraq War. By helping Turkey defeat Kurdish militias, Iran had hoped to win Ankara's favor at the expense of its own archenemy, Washington. But Iran flipped this posture in 2011, and by making peace with Kurdish militants it gave the PKK freedom to target Turkey.[15]

The new stance on the PKK would not have worked so well against Turkey had the Syrian uprising not excited Kurds across the Middle East. As rebels eroded the Assad regime's power in northern Syria in 2012, Kurds started taking control of cities there, just across the border with Turkey.

Encouraged by this development, the PKK tried to wrest control of Turkish towns, targeting especially vulnerable spots in the rugged and isolated southernmost province, Hakkari, which borders Iraq and Iran.[16] Iran was seemingly complicit in this new PKK assault, at least in part. In August 2012 Turkish deputy prime minister Bulent Arinc told reporters that the government had "received information that [PKK] terrorists infiltrated from the Iranian side of the border" before launching a massive assault on the town of Semdinli in Hakkari.[17] Tehran denied this.

Rejuvenated by its welcome in Syria and Iran, and also by Ankara's stunted "Kurdish Opening" (an aborted effort in 2009 that had aimed to improve Kurds' rights in Turkey) the PKK made a big push. In August 2012 the group killed nine people with a car bomb in Gaziantep, a prosperous and mixed Turkish-Kurdish city that had been spared from PKK violence. Once again the Syrian-Iranian axis cast its shadow over the assault: Turkish officials alleged Syrian complicity in the Gaziantep attack, and when Iranian nuclear negotiator Saeed Jalili met with Turkey's prime minister in Istanbul on September 18, he was also reportedly admonished.[18]

Ankara's Middle East policy rests on one basic premise: anyone who supports the PKK is Turkey's enemy. This means Ankara has a problem with Damascus until Assad falls, and a long-term problem with Tehran even afterward. Turkey may be able to turn the tables on both these rivals by solidifying a political accord with the PKK. In March 2013 the PKK's long-imprisoned leader, Abdullah Ocalan, announced his support for a cease-fire and a process of demilitarization of the conflict. A lasting peace would neutralize the "Kurdish card" that Turkey's rivals have long played when they wished to push back against Turkish regional ambitions.

These shifting sands in the Middle East have also brought Ankara closer to its longtime ally, the United States. This was demonstrated by Turkey's recent decision to host NATO's missile defense system, which aims to protect members of the Western alliance from Iranian and other nuclear threats.

This has all been possible because the AKP has come to realize that its strategic value as a Muslim power resides in its strong ties to the United States and access to NATO technology and muscle. Of course, other factors have helped foster Ankara's foreign policy change. The close relationship that has emerged between Prime Minister Erdogan and President Barack Obama is important in this regard. The Turkish leader appears to have a penchant for personal friendship with other foreign leaders, and Obama has given him attention and respect, which in turn encouraged the remolding of Turkish foreign policy through Erdogan's powerful personality. Starting in 2010 the two leaders spoke with each other often—at least a dozen times in 2011, with Erdogan reportedly getting nearly as many phone calls from the White House that year as did the British prime minister, the most frequent receiver of overseas calls from the White House.

It took time and hard work to get to this point. Before 2010 Turkey's relationship with Washington had been wavering due to Ankara's oscillating policy on Iran, which often challenged Washington's efforts to impose internationally backed sanctions on Tehran.

In June 2010, for example, Turkey voted at the UN Security Council against a proposal for U.S.-sponsored sanctions. For about two months it looked as though this vote would severely strain U.S.-Turkish ties. But the straightforward conversation Obama had with Erdogan on the sidelines of the July G20 summit in Toronto changed everything. The U.S. president repeatedly told Erdogan how upsetting Turkey's UN vote had been to him, and his candor helped clear the air between the two, as Turkish and U.S. officials and friends have told me. And Turkey's policy soon changed. Ankara went radio silent on Tehran's nuclear ambitions and began working with Washington.

Since then Obama and Erdogan seem to have really hit it off: Turkish media outlets reported that after Erdogan's mother died in 2011, Obama was among the world leaders who called him, and that the two "spoke for 45 minutes about their feelings."[19] This personal rapport is the foundation of the new U.S.-Turkish relationship.

So, after a tumultuous ten-year road and amid the instability of the Arab Spring, Turkey has managed to blend a pro-U.S. foreign policy line with its new Muslim sensitivities. This has been a major foreign policy move by the Turkish government. If the Cold War defined NATO's identity in the twentieth century, then the missile defense project perhaps defines NATO in the twenty-first. Just as members of the alliance agreed to defend one another against communism during the Cold War with the missile defense project, the members of NATO have now agreed to defend one another against a new threat, namely ballistic missiles that would likely come from Iran, Russia, China, or other volatile regions.

This is what makes Ankara's decision to join the missile defense system the most important Turkish foreign policy move of the last decade. It is Turkey saying that Ankara's relations with the West remain key, but more important that Turkey now appreciates the effect its Western overlay—that is, NATO membership—will have in making it a regional power.

For the Saudis and other Arab nations in the Middle East, Turkey is no longer a "wealthy Yemen" but rather is the strong Turkey that Ankara sought to be when it launched its Middle East policy a decade ago.

TABLE 3. Turkish Airlines Destinations Served from Istanbul, 1999–2010

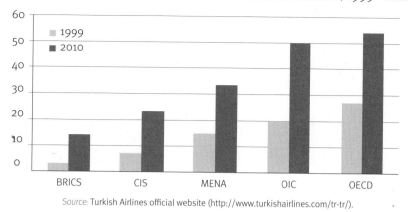

Source: Turkish Airlines official website (http://www.turkishairlines.com/tr-tr/).

BUT STILL AWAY FROM EUROPE

Even if Turkey has pivoted back to the United States, this is not to say that the new Turkey will also try to refit into Europe. The best way to describe the new Turkey is as a "Eurasian China"—a country that is aggressively trading with the entire world while building connections to distant destinations. This is best demonstrated by a comparison of the number of direct destinations served from Istanbul by the country's flagship carrier, Turkish Airlines, in 1999 and 2010.

In other words, whereas the old Turkey fell almost neatly under the European rubric, the new Turkey, which does business and forges diplomatic and societal ties with the entire world, does not. In this regard Turkey is a "Muslim BRICS" that has made a pivot toward the United States. For the "Eurasian China" model to be sustainable, however, the Turkish economy must keep humming along and the country's politics must remain relatively stable.

This is where foreign policy comes in: Turkey has demonstrated relative stability at a time when the region around it has been in upheaval. This, in turn, attracts investment from less stable neighbors like Iran, Iraq, and Syria. Ultimately, political stability and regional clout are Turkey's hard cash. Its economic growth and ability to rise as a "Muslim BRICS" and "Eurasian China" will depend on both.

5 | Beyond Ottoman Benevolence

The use of the term *Turk* in modern Turkey is a puzzling phenomenon. People in Turkey see all Muslims as Turks, regardless of their ethnicity or language. This means that not only ethnic Turks but also other groups such as Kurds, Circassians, and Bosnians are regarded as Turks, while non-Muslims (including Armenians and Jews) are not, even when they speak Turkish and are citizens of the country. This is not simply a matter of semantics: in Turkey, being a Turk has tangible benefits. Since only Turks are full members of the nation and considered loyal citizens, this perception is key to joining mainstream society. On the other hand not being regarded as a Turk leads to the stigma of being an imperfect citizen. Despite the fact that the contemporary Turkish constitution of 1982 defines all inhabitants of the country as Turks, in reality, non-Muslims (a term used collectively to refer to Jews and Christians who make up less than 1 percent of the country's population) are not viewed as Turks.[1] For instance, they are informally barred from becoming government employees, diplomats, or army officers.

Many Muslim Turks and Turkey's officially secular government routinely marginalize Jews and Christians. Furthermore, public antagonism, especially toward Christians, can be virulent and is often unchallenged. Controversy involving Turkish-Protestant churches is a case in point. News stories have appeared in the press since the late 1990s documenting the proliferation of small grassroots churches in the major cities. An immediate nationalist public backlash ensued. The fact that these churches were mostly started by Turkish converts was ignored, and the public excoriated foreign missionaries for proselytizing. Christianity was portrayed as unfit for Muslim Turks, who would not have converted were it not for Christian missionary manipulation.[2]

Christianity is viewed as alien by Turkish society in general, a painful situation for the country's small Christian communities. The Ottoman Empire was a multiethnic and multireligious state, however, and the empire separated its citizens into religious compartments, known as *millets*. This produced a stable social system that lasted around half a millennium. Although the *millet* system provided for religious freedoms for the members of the recognized Orthodox, Muslim, Jewish, and Armenian *millets*—later various other Christian denominations would also be organized as separate *millets*—it also left an indelible religious marker across the Balkans and in modern Turkey, core territories of the Ottoman Empire. It is not surprising that in the nineteenth century when the empire melted down during the age of nationalisms, Ottoman peoples in these areas imagined nationalism not as an ethnic but rather as an ethno-religious community. Therefore the empire collapsed along ethno-religious (*millet*) lines in the nineteenth century. This pitted the Ottoman Muslims against the Ottoman Christians. And when the rump Ottoman Muslim *millet* coalesced into the modern Turkish nation, Turkish nationalism embraced all Muslims in Turkey as Turks, while Christians were left outside of the body of the Turkish nation. Since Turkish ethnicity was seen as conterminous with Ottoman Muslim ethnicity (i.e., Balkan–Anatolian–Black Sea Muslims), Ottoman Christians have been excluded from the Turkish nation, even when they spoke Turkish. It is high time for Turkey to move beyond this legacy.

Bursa, the first capital city of the Ottoman Empire and the place where the Ottomans invented the *millet* system in the early fourteenth century, brings together the Ottoman legacy and today's reality regarding Christians and Jews. This former Ottoman imperial city, now home to nearly 2 million inhabitants, also hosts a number of important early Ottoman monuments, including the tomb of Osman I, the founder of the Ottoman Empire and its first sultan. When Osman I died in the early fourteenth century, his son and successor, Orhan, had him buried in an Eastern Orthodox monastery in Bursa.[3] With this act of brilliant statecraft, Orhan kicked off a multi-religious vision for the emerging Ottoman Empire. He paved the way for the integration of the Christian and Jewish populations of the withering Byzantine Empire into his state, catapulting the Ottomans to empire and, after its conquest in 1453, transforming Istanbul into a cosmopolitan metropolis.

In due course the Ottoman Empire expanded into Europe, incorporating numerous European peoples, from Greeks to Poles to Hungarians and Spanish Jews. As the empire became multiethnic, so did its capital. By the sixteenth century, Istanbul, with over a million inhabitants, was the largest city in the world. It also boasted a multilingual and multireligious population, including Italians, Greeks, Croats, Serbs, Bosnians, Germans, Spanish Jews, and Armenians, as well as Ottoman Turks.

This early Ottoman reality is now all but forgotten in modern Turkey, overtaken by the legacy of the nineteenth century Ottoman Empire that pitted Christians and Muslims against each other. This explains modern Turkey's twentieth-century hostility toward Christians and, with the recent rise of anti-Semitism in the country, also toward the Jews. Even though Turkey has moved to a post-Kemalist phase as Ataturk's political vision is transformed by the AKP, the Turkish views of Christians and Jews have yet to move into the twenty-first century.

Turkey's newfound fascination with its Ottoman past is evident in the groundswell of television programs, films, and books that romanticize the Ottoman era and attempt to link today's rising Turkey with the former glory of the Ottomans. This new way of thinking is more than just nostalgia—it colors the way Turks see themselves today and reshapes how Turkey imagines its role in the Middle East.

OTTOMANIA IS NOT THE FIX TO THE
CHRISTIAN AND JEWISH INEQUALITY PROBLEM

This new worldview is often portrayed as a refreshing way to reimagine Turkish identity and negate Kemalism's side effects that have led to systematic injustice against Christians and Jews. Yet, this idealistic picture of a just society clashes with the continuing daily realities of discrimination against Turkey's Christian and Jewish minorities. To its credit, Turkey's pre-republican past does provide a useful, if fantastical, canvass upon which to paint a picture of harmony between different creeds and ethnicities. But neo-Ottomanism also poses its own dangers to liberal democracy. The Ottoman political order that many Turks so revere may have been tolerant for its day, but it is not a replacement for the ideals of modern egalitarian societies. In fact, it conceals its own prejudices. After all, the rights that minorities enjoyed under the Ottomans were not of the sort possessed by today's emancipated citizens. Rather, they were part of a rigidly hierarchical social order that—while it protected minorities—did not accord them equal status as citizens.

The new Turkey's excited embrace of its imagined Ottoman heritage was most recently demonstrated by the millions of people who flocked to the movie theaters to see *The Conquest 1453*, an action extravaganza that adopted many of the stylistic aspects of Hollywood blockbusters like *300*. As this film illustrates, Turkey's "return to the past" has little to do with fidelity to historical fact. Rather, the rising Ottomania is laden with contemporary accretions, such as commercialism and political neo-Ottomanism.

One of these trends is Ottoman Islamic consumerism. This trend creates its appeal by characterizing the Ottomans as a religious civilization that resonates with conservative sensibilities, and this Ottoman revivalism is increasingly being adopted by Turkey's newly moneyed conservative elite. Safak Cak, an Istanbul-based designer, says Islamic consumerism "explains why some people are busy designing mansions with specially arranged praying rooms and Swarovski-covered toilet seats."

Consumerist and conservative Ottoman revivalism is not just limited to interior design. Turkey now has a number of "Islamic" summer resorts, with baroque Ottoman architecture, state-of-the-art services, and separate facilities for men and women.

The rise of Ottoman revivalism is Kemalism's demise in reverse. For decades, visitors to Turkey were treated to "Ataturk-mania"—statues and portraits of Turkey's founder, Kemal Ataturk, were sprinkled across the country, from airports and schools to hotels and homes. Now medieval Ottoman calligraphy, indecipherable to most Turks but undoubtedly Islamic in character, is replacing the fixation on Ataturk. Ottoman Islamic consumerism sells a simple message: Never mind who the Ottomans really were, just buy their symbols.

Subsequently, neo-Ottomanism is becoming the political lens through which many Turks view world politics. *The Conquest 1453* best exemplifies this trend. Armed with plenty of artistic license, including an imaginary Turkish female chief engineer whose skills help the Ottomans breech the walls of Constantinople, the movie casts Ottomans and contemporary Turks as a superior but tolerant people, enjoying their global power status.

After showing two hours of fighting between medieval Turks and Greeks, *1453* nevertheless ends with a contemporary, albeit neo-Ottomanist, political message. Having just conquered Istanbul from the Greeks, victorious Ottoman Sultan Mehmed II marches into the Aya Sofya (Haghia Sophia), hugs a little Christian girl, and promises a grand message of "a world of Muslim-Christian coexistence, to be managed by the Turks." The French paper *Le Figaro* also sees the film as confirming the rise of political Ottomanism, saying, "The huge enthusiasm for this epic [film] is an indication of the wave of Ottomania that has affected Turkey in recent times."

TURKEY'S "FIRST CHRISTIAN"

Amid news of Turkey's reinvented Ottoman take on Jews and Christians (a progressive stance for its period that would be considered illiberal today), a key development has almost gone unnoticed. In 2011 the Turks elected the country's first Christian deputy, Erol Dora, to the Turkish parliament. Dora's election to the Turkish legislature, representing the Kurdish nationalist Peace and Democracy Party (BDP) is a true breath of fresh air. Not counting a handful of Christians who were allocated legislative seats in the twentieth century due to legal quotas, Dora is the first Christian deputy elected to sit in the Ankara legislature. This is big news, for Christians represent just barely greater than 1/1000 of the country's population. In a symbolic move Muslim Turks have chosen to elect a Christian Turk to represent them. This development presents an opportunity for Turkey to come to terms with its rich Christian heritage. Moreover, it signals that the country's opposed camps, clustered around the conservative AKP and its liberal-secular opponents in an almost homogenously Muslim Turkey, can learn to live together under a liberal roof.

The first element of symbolism in Dora's election is that he has de facto become the "First Christian" in Turkey, which was, as many say, the first country in history to have a Christian majority. During the Turkish republican experience, Turkish Christians have dwindled in numbers, and the country's Christian heritage weathered a tumultuous and debilitating period in the late nineteenth and early twentieth centuries. Now, with Dora in the parliament, Christian heritage in Turkey has found a voice, as well as a reminder of the country's thriving, and once dominant, Christian past.

However, the symbolism of Dora's election does not stop there. Dora faces a tall order, whether or not he is aware of it. First, he has been elected to the Turkish parliament representing a Kurdish nationalist party. His party, the BDP, does not hide its sympathies for the PKK, which until recently employed violence and terror attacks. And it gets even more complicated: in fact, Dora is neither Turkish nor Kurdish, but rather an ethnic Syriac. He embodies every dichotomy facing Turkey: Kurdish versus Turkish, Christian versus Muslim, secular versus conservative, Islamist versus liberal, and political activism versus violence.

Yet he also presents a political example showing the way forward for Turkey. Turkey has to provide for immediate constitutional equality for all its citizens, regardless of religion, especially since religion is such a strong marker of Turkishness in the country. To become a regional and potentially global power, Turkey must prove that as a Muslim-majority land, it is ready to treat all its citizens equally, especially its smallest religious communities.

6 | The Other Turkey

In Turkey's most recent elections, held in 2011, the AKP received 49.9 percent of the vote. To put it differently, whereas nearly half of the country voted for the governing party, the other half did not. "Turkey's other half" came out in force during the June 2013 "Gezi Protests," as urban, middle-class, secular, and liberal Turks took to the streets to protest the ruling party's violation of democratic principles and percieved interference in the lifestyles of secular-minded individuals. A tour around Izmir, Turkey's third largest city and a bastion of support for secularist opposition CHP, is a great opportunity to observe "the other Turkey" that falls outside the AKP's political umbrella. Excluding the 12.9 percent of the voters who supported the conservative Nationalist Action Party (MHP) and 1.25 percent who voted for the Islamist Felicity Party (SP) in the 2011 elections, in addition to the 49.9 percent who picked the AKP, the "other Turkey"—secularist, Kemalist (although lately increasingly liberal), and standing for a strict separation of religion and politics—accounts for around 35 percent of the population.

Izmir, with over 3 million citizens, is the "capital of the other Turkey" for all practical purposes. A walk around the palm tree–lined streets of this port city, founded as Smyrna by the ancient Greeks, is as iconoclastic a tour as it gets about clichés of the new Turkey that the AKP has forged. Izmir is a far cry from Turkish cities such as Kayseri that represent the new Turkey—devout, socially conservative, suffused with outward signs of religiously, and driven by the Anatolian Tiger zeal. Compared to Kayseri, a male in Izmir is half as likely to go to a mosque at least once a week, and those in Izmir are only one-third as likely to pray five times a day and fast at least thirty days a year. Izmir has the lowest percentage of people who believe restaurants should be closed down during Ramadan (21 percent) and those who believe that if religion and science conflict, religion is always correct (66 percent). In short, Izmir ranks lowest in the country in religiosity.[1]

This contrasts sharply with the average city in Turkey. Overall in Turkey 85 percent of the people define themselves as "religious," 71 percent pray, and 46 percent of this group pray five times a day; 86 percent of the population fasts, 72 percent of which say they fast during the entire month of Ramadan. Moreover, on issues of gender equality, Turkey is still very much the traditional patriarchal society: 33 percent of Turks think that a university education is more important for men than it is for women, 60 percent think that men should have priority for jobs over women in times of unemployment, 67 percent think that men make better administrators, and 71 percent think men are better political leaders than women.[2]

On the other hand, "the pearl of the Aegean" or "Infidel Izmir," as the city is sometimes called in Turkey depending on one's political proclivity, is a secularist haven and also a bastion of relative irreligiousness. Signs of conservative Turkey, such as the headscarf and disdain for alcohol, do not dominate here. The city's waterside promenade, known as the *kordon*, a street reminiscent of the Prom in Nice, is filled with people drinking and dining on seafood and couples on dates. As a BBC correspondent puts it, no place in Turkey clashes with the rise of conservatism more than Izmir, "where in the summer locals pack the nightclubs and the bars. Women wear miniskirts and low-cut tops here without a second thought. And there's alcohol."[3]

Izmir is a port city dominated by old money businesses that made their wealth selling Turkish sultanas, figs, olives, and tobacco to Europe and markets beyond since the seventeenth century. In other words, unlike Kayseri and Gaziantep, this city is neither new money nor an Anatolian Tiger. Izmir even challenges the conventional wisdom about the origins of the Turks. Unbeknownst to most outsiders, many of the city's inhabitants descend from European Muslim immigrants. The typical *Izmirli* looks more like their Slavic Muslim grandparent than like their Anatolian Turkic compatriots across the country in Kayseri. A little discussed fact among Turkey experts across the world and even among the country's citizens is that not all Turks are, well, Turks, and also that many of country's inhabitants are of immigrant origin. True, an overwhelming majority of the Turks are Muslims, and with the exception of some of the Kurds, an overwhelming majority of the country's inhabitants identify as Turks. But it is also true that almost half of the population is descended from Muslims who escaped religious persecution in Europe, and not all these people were ethnic Turks.

During the premodern era the Ottomans divided their population into strict religious compartments, the *millets*. Over five centuries the Ottoman *millet* system had transformed the ethnic identities of the Ottoman peoples into religious ones. This made one's membership in a certain *millet* the most significant factor of an Ottoman subject's identity. In the nineteenth century as the Balkan Christians turned to nationalism, their idea of ethnicity would hence be shaped by the *millet* system. Christian Ottoman *millets* in the Balkans developed into religio-national communities during the last phases of the Empire.[4] These Christian Ottoman *millets* did not see the Balkan Muslims as their nationals, even when the two communities shared languages.

Therefore, as the Christian states emerged in the Balkans during the territorial decline of the Ottoman Empire, Turkish and non-Turkish Muslims in southeastern Europe fled persecution in these newly emerging states, taking refuge in Anatolia and Thrace (modern Turkey). Among these immigrants were many Turks, but also Albanian, Bosnian, Croatian, Hungarian, Roma, Bulgarian, Macedonian, and Serbian Muslims. They were joined by Crimean Tatars, Circassians, Chechens, Georgians, Abkhazes, Daghestanis, and Ossetians, who fled Tzarist persecution as the Russian Empire expanded south, taking the Black Sea basin and the Caucasus from the Ottomans.

The demographic shift of these events was of epic dimensions. Justin McCarthy writes that between 1821 and 1922 five and a half million Ottoman Muslims were driven from their homes, while more than five million died in wars or of starvation and disease.[5] Kemal Karpat notes that between 1856 and 1914 more than seven million immigrants settled in Anatolia from various parts of the Ottoman Empire.[6]

Once in Anatolia, having been persecuted due to their religion, the surviving Ottoman Turkish Muslims unified around a common Turkish-Islamic identity. Moreover, the immigration of Ottoman Muslims to Anatolia enhanced the peninsula's Muslim and Turkish demographic base at the expense of its Christian communities.[7] During the nineteenth century about one-third of Anatolia's population was Christian. By 1913 the incoming Muslim populations had decreased the Christians' demographic weight to around one-fourth.[8] By the end of World War I, when Turkey and Greece decided to exchange their Greek Orthodox and Muslim minority populations, and following the deportation of Anatolian Armenians to Syria during the war, Turkey's population had become almost entirely Muslim, with the share of the non-Muslims in the country going down to 2.6 percent in 1927.[9]

Unsurprisingly, Turkish nationalism became an increasingly dominant ideology during this period among ethnic Turks and immigrant Muslims alike. The empire's collapse beneath the military might of the Allies during World War I had increased the Turkish-Muslim community's sense of vulnerability. As the war advanced, Anatolia had become especially important.[10] After the loss of the Balkans, when the Ottomans bid farewell to 69 percent of the country's population and 83 percent of its territory in Europe,[11] the Ottoman Empire became essentially a state of the Near East, with its territories stretching from Anatolia down to the Arabian Peninsula. During World War I the empire lost its Arab territories as well. The Turkish-Muslim community of Anatolia (and Thrace) was then convinced that Turkey was its only homeland.[12] Hence, following the defeat of the Ottoman Empire in World War I, immigrant Muslims passionately joined the Turks to support Mustafa Kemal Ataturk's Turkish nationalist campaign to liberate Turkey from Allied occupation.

After Turkey was liberated, the modern Turkish republic was born as a secular, nation-state to match Ataturk's vision. In the 1920s Ataturk moved to discard religion in order to focus on a voluntaristic, territorial, and political understanding of the nation. To this end Ataturk tried to temper religion's role in shaping national identity through secularism. He made Turkey officially a secular state in the 1920s, but Islam never disappeared. Having indelibly marked the Ottoman Muslim and Turkish identity for centuries, Islam remained a major vehicle for Turkish identity even as religious practice per se became less important in daily life due to secularization.

IMMIGRANTS FROM EUROPE

From the beginning, Turks and other Muslims hailing from the more prosperous parts of the Ottoman Empire in Europe—who had traditionally dominated the Ottoman state—enjoyed a head start over Anatolian Muslims in modern Turkey. The founding cadres of the republic, including Ataturk himself, who was born in Salonika (now in Greece), came mostly from Europe and Russia. These groups formed Turkey's ruling elite well into the 1960s. Izmir and Istanbul (until mass migration from Anatolia finally transformed its population stock in the 1980s) have come to represent this little debated but key component of Turkey.

These European-origin elites enjoyed a preponderance of power until democracy facilitated opposition to their secular ideology to emerge as a political force. By the 1970s reaction against secularism had an anti-elitist hue. In this regard the rise of Islamist parties—the National Salvation Party in the 1970s, the Welfare Party in the 1990s, and the AKP in 2002—are all rooted as much in political resentment against elitism as in rural conservative Anatolian umbrage to secularism. Meanwhile, the idea of secularism has remained alive in areas traditionally dominated by immigrants from Europe, such as Izmir, that have in turn emerged as a bastion of support for Ataturk's secularist CHP.

Izmir is not unique among Turkish cities with a strong secularist ethos and a stock of non-Turkish and Turkish immigrants from Europe. There are many towns, such as Ayvalik and Kirklareli, and even small villages in Western Turkey, that could be termed "mini Izmirs." Western Turkey, especially the Aegean and Marmara Sea provinces, parts of the Mediterranean and Black Sea coastlines, and Thrace, has historically received a vast proportion of European immigrants, as opposed to central or eastern Turkey, which lie further away from Europe. This is secular Turkey, also known as the "land of the CHP." A vast majority part of the CHP's votes, totaling 70.2 percent of the 11.1 million votes the party received in the 2011 elections, came from Turkish provinces along the western Black Sea, Mediterranean, Aegean coasts, Ankara, and Thrace. The party also performed well in Ankara, the capital city with a mostly secular citizenry, although many of them are not of European origin.

MIDDLE AND UPPER-CLASS VOTERS

In addition to voters in this region, middle-class and upper-middle-class voters make up a proportionately large part of CHP voters. Take for instance, Ankara's middle- and upper-middle-class borough of Cankaya. In the 2011 elections the CHP received 55 percent of the vote in Cankaya, far above Ankara-wide support for that party, which stood at 31 percent. As for the AKP, it received 55 percent of the vote in Ankara's Kecioren borough, a district of less wealthy voters and mostly recent central Anatolian immigrants to the city. In Kecioren, the AKP outperformed its Ankara-wide support, which stood at 49 percent. In Sincan and Pursaklar, examples of the immigrant and working-class sections of Ankara, the AKP won 64.4 percent and 74.9 percent of the votes, respectively. The same patterns were repeated in Istanbul and other large Turkish cities. In the 2011 elections, whereas the CHP received 31 percent of the overall votes in Istanbul, support for the party rose to 58, 46, and 57.5 percent in Kadikoy, Sisli, and Bakirkoy—all upper-class districts. Meanwhile, the AKP did much better in working lower-middle-class varos boroughs, overwhelmingly populated by recent immigrants from the eastern Black Sea Coast and central, eastern, and southeastern Anatolia, receiving 60 percent, 59 percent, and 58 percent of the vote in Bagcilar, Sultangazi, and Umraniye. These numbers are far above average citywide support for that party. The city's Catalca borough is indicative of how the Anatolian versus Balkan/European nature of the voting patterns dominates voter behavior. Although this district is also considered varos, populated mostly by the lower-middle-class and working inhabitants, its population mostly comprises immigrants from the Balkans, including many from Bulgaria. Accordingly the CHP performed better in Catalca than in other varos boroughs, getting 41.5 percent of the vote.[13]

Bursa, Turkey's fourth largest city, displays this pattern as well. Centuries ago Bursa acquired a reputation as a silk-making city after the secrets of the craft were smuggled from China to the Mediterranean world during the late Byzantine era. Lately, the city has emerged as the hub of Turkey's burgeoning automotive industry, becoming a major industrial hub and attracting many immigrants from poor eastern Turkey, including a large number of Kurds. In the heart of Bursa's upper-middle-class section is the district of Nilufer, which houses the city's established residents, many of whom trace their roots to European Muslims. Drive to the eastern outskirts of the city, and you will enter Yildirim, a district of recent arrivals from impoverished Kurdish areas in eastern Turkey. It is no surprise that while the AKP received only 40 percent of the vote in Nilufer, it was able to capture nearly 60 percent in the varos of Yildirim. Voting patterns in Bursa demonstrate the two large and occasionally overlapping voting blocks that support the CHP and AKP, respectively: Turks of Balkan origin and middle-class Turks mostly vote for the secularist CHP, and Anatolian Turks and Kurds from the lower-middle class and working classes mostly vote for the conservative AKP.

THE ALEVIS

There is one more voting block that supports the CHP, the Alevis, who constitute at least 10 percent of Turkey's population and profess a liberal understanding of Islam. Strong support for CHP and weak support for the AKP among the Alevis becomes overwhelmingly clear in north and east-central Turkey, the traditional heartland of Alevis in Turkey. Take, for instance, Tunceli's Ovacik district in which the CHP polled a skyrocketing 71.6 percent in 2011. The AKP received only 5 percent of the votes in Ovacik in the 2011 elections, a tellingly low turnout in a solidly Alevi district for the governing party. The level of strong support for the CHP in Ovacik also demonstrates support among Alevis across the board for that party. Ovacik is overwhelmingly Kurdish, and even if support for the CHP is rather weak among Kurds overall, Kurds in this poor yet nearly entirely Alevi district vote overwhelmingly for the CHP.

The strong Alevi preference for the CHP is also on display in the Arguvan district of Malatya and the Divrigi district of Sivas. Both these districts have large Turkish and also Kurdish Alevi populations. In 2011 the CHP polled 73 percent and 66 percent of the total vote in Arguvan and Divrigi, respectively. The AKP, on the other hand, received only 20 percent of the vote in Arguvan and 25 percent in Divrigi. The Alevis appear to be yet another part of the voting block forming the "other Turkey"—that is, the country's one-third unlikely to throw its support behind the AKP.

Why are the Alevis so committedly secularist? The answer to this question lies in the history of this group of uniquely Turkish form of Islam. The Alevis are originally from a triangular zone of north-central Anatolia, an area stretching from Eskisehir in the northwest to Erzurum in the northeast and Kahramanmaras in the south. In addition, smaller Alevi communities (called Cepnis, Tahtacis, Turkmens, or Yoruks) are spread on the mountain ranges along the Aegean and Mediterranean littorals, from Canakkale in northwestern Turkey to Gaziantep in southern Turkey. Depending on one's relationship to Islam, in Turkey the Alevis are described as Sufi Muslims, liberal Muslims, Sunni Muslims, Shiite Muslims, non-Muslims, or even as heretics (by fundamentalist Muslims). In reality, the Alevis are a distinct community whose interpretation of Islam, while showing similarities to both Sunni and Shiite Islam, is unorthodox enough to be considered neither Sunni nor Shiite.[14]

The exact number of Alevis in Turkey is difficult to verify because official statistics do not count ethnicity or religion. The polls that do deal with these subjects seem imperfect: because historically the Alevis have suffered persecution, many of them still shy away from self-identifying in polls. Some Alevi individuals and organizations, such as the Cem Foundation (*Cem Vakfi*), an Alevi NGO, claim that Alevis are nearly a third of Turkey's Muslim population, more than 20 million people, while others place this figure even higher at 25 million.[15] The U.S. State Department reports an "estimated fifteen to twenty million" Alevis in Turkey, comprising 20 to 28 percent of the Turkish population.[16]

These figures may, however, be overstated. A recent poll that used three indirect questions about Alevi iconography in homes, instead of directly asking whether the informant is an Alevi, concluded that the Alevis constitute 10.4 percent of the Turkish population.[17]

But again, this study may have neglected Alevis who are reluctant to divulge information about their private rituals. On balance it seems possible to estimate that the Alevis constitute at least 10 percent of the Turkish population. Given this number, together with secular Sunni Muslims, the Alevis can be said to constitute an important component of Turkey's secular block. The roots of the Alevis' support for secularism lie in their history, specifically the emergence of Alevism as a Turkish faith in Anatolia, and the political freedoms provided to them by Ataturk.

Alevism emerged as a specifically Turkish interpretation of Islam in medieval Turkey. The Turks' original homeland is northern Eurasia, where they practiced shamanism. During the early medieval period Chinese pressure pushed the Turks westward, first into Uzbekistan and then into Iran in the eighth century. At that time the Turks came into contact with the Islamic Umayyad and later Abbasid empires that ruled those areas. Over time many Turkish tribes became the soldiers of the caliphate in Baghdad. These contacts ushered in a process of gradual Islamization of the Turks. Slowly, over a period of two hundred years, the Turks became Muslims mostly through contact with the Persians, who at the time belonged to Sunni Islam.

In the eleventh century the Iranian-based Turkish Seljuk Empire captured most of Anatolia from the Byzantine Empire. The ensuing Seljuk state in Turkey was multiethnic and multi-religious, with Jewish and Christian (Greek, Syriac, and Armenian) populations who enjoyed religious tolerance. At this time Turkish Sufi movements born in Central Asia grew in the Anatolian cities, promoting liberal forms of Islam.

Not surprisingly, the Sufis and medieval Turkish humanist groups and thinkers, such as the Mevlevis (Whirling Dervishes who follow Rumi), the Bektasis, and Yunus Emre, who emphasized faith at the expense of practice in Islam, were accepting of the Anatolian Christians. In this tolerant environment of Seljuk Anatolia, a synthesis of Islam and Christianity created an open, urban form of Islam that borrowed much from Christianity, including a fundamental Sufi concept, the veneration of saints.

This uniquely Turkish form of urban Islam was enhanced by the arrival of a new wave of Turks from Central Asia in the early thirteenth century. These Turkish tribes, fleeing the Mongols, were shamanist, as had been the earlier waves of Turkish tribes before they left their homeland.

The previous Turks, however, had been gradually filtered through Iran as well as urbanized and Islamized by the Persians. This slow process had given these Turks plenty of time to adjust to their new faith, switching from the free tribal spirit of shamanism to the stricter mores and values of Islam. In contrast the thirteenth-century Turkish tribes were catapulted into Anatolia almost overnight. They had only a few years to acculturate to Islam, a process for which the previous wave of Turks had had centuries.

With the ensuing culture shock, the shamanistic Turks in Anatolia found the liberal Sufi version of Islam closer to their taste than orthodox Islam. They also chose to preserve parts of their shamanistic culture, such as dance and music in worship and mixed-gender prayers. The cross-pollination of Sufi Islam and shamanism produced a specific version of rural Turkish Islam, initially called *kizilbas* (a term that later became pejorative and remains so to this day despite efforts by some Alevis to appropriate it) and later named Alevism. This Turkish form of Islam avoided some aspects of Sunni Islam, such as the separation of men and women in prayer. The Alevis' unorthodox take on mainstream Islam also meant that religious service was not held in a mosque. Rather, such worship took place in a *cemevi* (house of gathering) or any place available when the Alevis faced persecution. Worship was run not by an imam but by a *dede* (elder). Prayers were conducted in Turkish

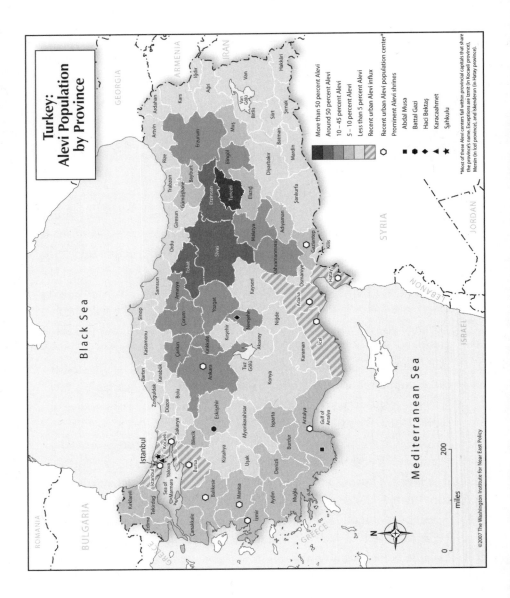

Map 2. Alevi population by province in Turkey.
Courtesy of the Washington Institute for Near East Policy.

rather than Arabic, which renders the Alevis the only Muslims able to pray in the vernacular. Dancing and wine drinking, rooted in shamanism, and oratory celebrations also became common in the Alevi faith. In the open nature of medieval Turkish Anatolia, Alevism became a popular form of Islam across the countryside, supplementing that of the urban Sufis. In this regard, a fair amount of mixing took place between the Sufis and Alevis. For instance, the Bektasis gradually became a Sufi order influenced by Alevism, while Alevis incorporated elements of Bektasism, such as veneration of saints.

As the Anatolian Seljuks gave way to the Ottoman Empire, and the Ottomans expanded into the Balkans, the Sufis, Bektasis, and Alevis moved into Europe, forming today's Alevi/Bektasi communities in the Balkans, such as the Alevi Turks in Bulgaria and Greece, as well as the Bektasis in Albania, who constitute about a quarter of that country's population. During their expansion into Europe, the Ottomans made the Bektasis the official religious order of the janissaries, the elite corps of the imperial army. This development succeeded in co-opting the Balkan Christians, attracting many of them into the Ottoman army by making it easy for them to become Muslims yet avoid the orthodox practice of Islam if they wished.

In the late fifteenth century, however, the Alevis found themselves caught in a battle for power between the Ottoman state, whose Muslim population was predominantly Sunni, and Safavid Iran, which became an officially Shiite state in 1502 under the reign of Shah Ismail I. The most divisive historical issue between the Sunnis and the Shiites is the question of the succession following the death of the Muslim prophet Muhammad. Whereas the Shiites asserted that Prophet Muhammad's state should be run by his son-in-law Ali, the Sunnis rejected this point. Gradually, some Shiites became entrenched in their devotion to Ali. In the early sixteenth century Shiite Iran sent emissaries into Anatolia, spreading the idea of veneration of Ali in an effort to gain political muscle vis-à-vis the Sunni Ottoman state. The Alevis were ostensibly attracted by this policy because they were already at home with the idea of veneration of saints and prominent figures of Islam, including Ali. Despite their respect for Ali and the affinity they may have felt to

Turkic-run Iran, however, the Alevis did not convert to Shiism, largely because for the unorthodox Alevis, Shiism, an orthodox form of Islam, was akin to the Sunni Islam, which they avoided.

Nevertheless, the Ottoman sultans, wary of Iranian expansion into eastern Turkey, saw the Alevis' devotion to Ali as a sign of Shiite heresy—a fifth-column for Persia. The Ottoman response to this perceived threat was massive persecution of the Alevis. Especially under the rule of Sultan Selim I (Yavuz) in the early sixteenth century, many Alevis were killed. Others were expelled to Iran or fled there for safety (where they merged with Turkic Shiite Azeris). Subsequently the Ottoman sultans secured eastern Turkey. The Alevis survived far from the Iranian border, in the refuge of the high mountains of inner Anatolia. Fearing persecution, the Alevis spent the ensuing centuries in rural mountain hamlets where they could hide their religious practices and try to pass as Sunni Muslims when necessary to avoid maltreatment.

When the Ottoman sultans obliterated the janissaries in 1826, replacing the corps with the new Western army, they also banned Bektasism, closely associated with the janissaries. Like the Alevis, the Bektasis were forced to go underground. Gradually, the experience of persecution and survival in disguise brought the Alevis and Bektasis closer to each other than before, and some Bektasis started to self-identify as the urban branch of Alevism. The two groups, however, largely remained on the margins of the Ottoman society until Ataturk, whose vision for a secular republic included the emancipation of the Alevis and Bektasis.

ALEVI SUPPORT FOR SECULARISM

Secularization and elimination of Islam as a state religion under Ataturk drastically altered the situation of the Alevis and the Bektasis. Almost overnight these people went from persecuted "heretics" to first-class citizens of the republic. Eventually many Alevis moved from the mountain hamlets where they had lived since the 1500s to the cities. This process, coupled with mass secular education, enabled the Alevis to move into Turkish society and up its social and economic ladders. Especially significant in this period, thousands of Alevis, including many women educated as early as the 1930s, became schoolteachers in Turkey's secular education system, spreading the idea of a secular republic.

Liberation and a taste of equality under Ataturk meant that the Alevis built up a strong devotion to Ataturk and his legacy. Today in many Alevi homes, especially in the countryside, pictures of Ataturk hang next to pictures of Ali (from whom the Alevis get their name), an iconic statement showing the elevated status of the founder of modern Turkey among the Alevis.

The Alevis showed loyalty not only to Ataturk but also to his party, the CHP. Starting in the 1960s the Alevis threw their support heavily behind leftist as well as communist movements and political parties with which they identified as a historically persecuted group. When the CHP moved to the left in the 1960s, the Alevis supported this process. In the 1970s the Alevis played a significant role in setting up socialist and communist unions, political parties, militias, and even terrorist groups.

As a result of their identification with communism and secularism, the Alevis became the targets of Islamists, as well as of Turkish nationalist parties that promoted an anti-Russian, hence anticommunist, ideology during the Cold War. In the chaotic years of intra-militia violence in the 1970s the Alevis were targeted by these groups. During one such event in 1978, in Kahramanmaras, militia and sympathizers of Islamist and nationalist parties killed more than a hundred Alevis, wounding more than a thousand others. Violent clashes in Corum, Sivas, and Malatya in the late 1970s led to similar pogroms in which Alevi neighborhoods were attacked and businesses burned.

The Alevis' political tendencies have changed somewhat since the 1970s. With the collapse of communism, many have moved away from that ideology. Some have even shown support for center-right political parties, such as the ANAP. Today the CHP still attracts many Alevis, although more among rural populations. Meanwhile, some Alevis seem to support the Turkish nationalist MHP.

Despite fluctuating political affiliations, the Alevis have remained steadfast in their devotion to a secular Turkey, resisting Islamism and social conservatism. In fact, among all the pillars supporting secularism in Turkey, the Alevis may be the only ones not weakened by the

TABLE 4. Alevi Self-Identification (figures rounded)

Muslim only	12 percent
Muslim and Alevi	32 percent
Alevi only (including Bektasi and Kizilbas)	41 percent
Atheist*	15 percent

*Includes Alevis who responded "human being" (0.5 percent).

Source: Kamil Fırat, "Kentleşen Alevilik" (Urbanizing Alevism), quoted in *Milliyet*,
July 5, 2005. http://www.milliyet.com.tr/2005/07/05/guncel/guno1.html.

AKP. In this regard the Alevis continue to have a persistent exclusivist self-perception regarding Islam in politics. According to a recent poll conducted by the Middle East Technical University (ODTU) in Ankara, for instance, while only 12 percent of the Alevis saw themselves as "exclusively Muslims," 32 percent identified as "both Alevi and Muslim," 34.5 percent as "only Alevis," and 6 percent as "Bektasi" or "Kizilbas." Moreover, a large number of Alevis now seem entirely secular or irreligious. In the ODTU poll 15.1 percent (more than those who self-identified as "only Muslims") said they were "atheist" (see figure 1).[18]

Meanwhile, the Islamists conservative politicians, the AKP, and the Alevis seem to have trouble coming together. Accordingly, the Alevis have been markedly absent from Turkey's Islamist and religion-based parties. Only a few Alevi deputies exist among the more than 327 deputies of the governing AKP in the Turkish parliament, despite the fact that the Alevis constitute over 10 percent of the Turkish population.

Today, a large number of Alevis live in Istanbul, Ankara, and other major cities where they have migrated since Ataturk. Intensive migration from cities in east-central Turkey following the pogroms of the 1970s has diminished the ratio of Alevis in towns such as Sivas, Kahramanmaras, and Malatya. Nevertheless, large numbers of Alevis still live in the rural areas of these provinces and others across north-central, central, and east-central Turkey, although Tunceli is the only Turkish province where the Alevis constitute a significant majority (over 60 percent) of the population.

As with the rest of Turkish society, the 1980s witnessed the emergence of a large middle class among the Alevis. Over time the Alevis have integrated into Turkish society, and intermarriages between Alevis and Sunni Turks have become common. Still, during a 1993 Alevi cultural festival in Sivas, organized partly by Alevis and partly by left-wing groups, Sunni fundamentalists set fire to the hotel where the delegates were staying, burning alive thirty-five people under the eyes of police and security forces, who later came under heavy criticism for their failure to act. The incident served as a warning to some Alevis that at least a residual dislike for them remains in parts of Turkey, although the social stigma by Sunnis toward Alevis (such as the common allegation that Alevis engaged in incest) has subsided somewhat in recent years.

Partly in reaction to the Sivas incident, a revivalist movement emerged in the 1990s among urban Alevis. The movement culminated in the establishment of a number of NGOs that promote Alevi identity. The revivalist efforts have, however, been met with limited success. Given massive secularization among the Alevis since Ataturk and the drift away from theology under the influence of leftist movements since the 1960s, the Alevi religious traditions, kept and taught orally to avoid persecution, are now for the most part forgotten and in some cases entirely lost. Moreover, while older generations see Alevism as a matter of faith, younger people call it a philosophy, leading a very large number of young Alevis not to identify as Muslims. According to the previously mentioned ODTU poll, among people born after 1965, some 30.1 percent consider themselves "atheist," and a mere 2.5 percent identify as "Muslims." Among the same group, 37 percent see themselves as "Alevis," 22 percent as "both Alevi and Muslim," and 8.5 percent as "Kizilbas" or "Bektasi" (see figure 2). Moreover, compared to older Alevis (i.e., those born before 1965), younger Alevis (i.e., those born after 1965) are more than seven times less likely to identify as "Muslim." More important, the younger Alevis are more than eleven times more likely to identify as "Atheist" compared to the older Alevis. Secularization seems to be the future of Alevism in Turkey.

Women

Middle-class and educated women have been the leading beneficiaries of Turkish secularism, and as such this group is a part of the "other

TABLE 5. Generational Difference in Alevi
Self-Identification (figures rounded)

Self-Identification	Born Category of	
	1964 or earlier	1965 or later
Muslim only	17 percent	2.5 percent
Muslim and Alevi	41.5 percent	22 percent
Alevi only (including Bektasi and Kizilbas)	38 percent	46 percent
Atheist*	3.5 percent	30 percent

*Includes Alevis who responded "human being" (0.9 percent).

Source: Kamil Fırat, "Kentleşen Alevilik" (Urbanizing Alevism), quoted in Milliyet,
July 5, 2005. http://www.milliyet.com. tr/2005/07/05/guncel/gun01.html.

Turkey," secularist block that has thus far refused to support the AKP. As a result of political equality granted by Ataturk in the 1930s and early access to higher education, today women are represented heavily in the country's professional classes: 40 percent of all teachers in Turkey are women, as are 35 percent of all engineers, 30 percent of all doctors, 25 percent of all college professors, and 33 percent of all lawyers.[19] Still, women have had little access to political power in Turkey in the past decade. According to a 2010 report by IRIS Group to Observe Equality, an Ankara-based women's rights group, of the 139 director-generals in the country responsible for running government agencies or departments, only 8 were women, representing 5.7 percent of bureaucrats at this level. There was only 1 woman among the 254 regional directors of ministries, representing 0.4 percent of top bureaucrats at this level, and only 22 of the 942 provincial directors appointed by the AKP were women, representing 2.3 percent of all such directors.

Similarly a 2010 report by the Turkish prime minister's Office of Personnel showed that women have been nearly nonexistent in the upper echelons of Turkish bureaucracy. Only 2 (Nimet Çubukcu and Selma Aliye Kavaf) of the 26 ministers in the Turkish cabinet were women—one was responsible for education, and the other was in charge of women's affairs. Moreover, there were no women among the 25 undersecretaries appointed by the AKP. Of the 85 deputy undersecretaries, only 3 were women, representing merely 3.5 percent of all bureaucrats at this level.[20]

Professional, educated, and middle-class women have hence become at least part of the bloc opposing the governing party. In 2007, for instance, when a number of anti-AKP and pro-secularist demonstrations rocked Turkey, women appeared to dominate these rallies. Likewise, middle-class, educated women played a prominent role in the 2013 anti-AKP demonstrations. According to press reports, women constituted the majority of the 1.2 million demonstrators in Istanbul who attended an anti-AKP rally in April 2007.[21] Moreover, all nine members of the committee coordinating the country-wide demonstrations at that time were women. With a number of educated women appearing to be uncomfortable with the AKP, this completes the profile of the "other Turkey": educated women (especially those with college-level and advanced degrees), middle- and upper-middle-class voters, Alevis (including working and lower-middle-class voters, as well as Kurds) and Turkish citizens of European origin.

SPLIT TURKEY

These secular constituents are increasingly having to cope with new demographic and political realities in Turkey that are changing the electoral landscape and remolding national politics. Having emerged from its population boom nearly two decades ago, Turkey is now undergoing another demographic transformation. Many Turks in rural areas and small towns are migrating to large cities and coastal Turkey to look for jobs and attend school or simply to obtain better services. Settling in outlying areas and varos neighborhoods, these newcomers are much more receptive to the AKP than to the secular establishment as represented by the CHP. And so these metropolitan areas—once bastions of the secular Turkey—are becoming the new battlegrounds in a two-way race between the secularist CHP and the Islamist-rooted AKP.[22] This new pattern of competition is further polarizing the political debate in Turkey, widening the chasm between the AKP and the CHP on a range of issues.

Moreover, this political polarization is exacerbated by attitudes of intolerance on social issues. Istanbul's Bahcesehir University conducted a study on social attitudes in Turkey, using an eighteen-question survey to access the level of conservative views held by respondents. The study found that on a scale of 1 to 100, "infidel" Izmir scores 52 and Turkey's other European-influenced coastal zones score 59. Compare this to Turkey's Anatolian heartland, which score from the mid-60s to the low 70s on the scale of conservatism. These cleavages are evident across the gambit of social issues. For instance, there is a clear divide regarding views on women's roles in the family. The poll asked Turkish women if in a marriage the wife should "always submit to her husband, and never defy him." In Izmir the percentage of women in agreement with this claim was consistently below 40 percent. In Turkey's Anatolian stretches, however, women often agree with this claim, with agreement rates between 68 percent and 71 percent.

Turkey has always been a relatively conservative country, and conservatism (as measured by views on religion, women's status and rights, family, political ideology, nationalism, sexual freedom, authoritarian tendencies, and free will versus fate) seems to be a long-term trend in the country. In the Bahcesehir study that measured these attitudes on a scale of 1 to 100, Turkey's conservatism score was 60.34 in 1990 and 63.00 in 2011. The biggest difference over the years has been in the conservatism of college graduates, whose rates of conservatism have jumped from 38.5 to 54.8.

By the same token Turkey appears to have become more Muslim in its identity in recent years. Those who primarily identified as Muslim comprised 36 percent of the population in 1999, whereas this number increased to 45 percent, almost half of the country, in 2006. This has also led to an increase in the percentage of the population who assert that parties should be able to practice politics on a basis of religion from 25 percent to 41 percent.

Despite the increase in prosperity and democratic reforms over the past decade, Turkish society does not appear to be growing more tolerant. Since the 1990s Turkey has consistently ranked rather low compared to other countries when it comes to tolerance of different lifestyles and identities. In 2011 Turkish social scientists sought to measure intolerance in Turkey by asking Turks which categories of people they would not want as neighbors.

The most unwanted neighbors in Turkey are gays, with 84 percent of those polled expressing that they would not want to live next to people who are gay. Next are those who have HIV; 74 percent of Turks stigmatize this group. Also, 68 percent of Turks would find unmarried couples who lived next to them undesirable. A full 64 percent would not want to live next to atheists, and 48 percent of Turks would not want to live next to Christians. Interestingly, this sort of intolerance seems to cut both ways in Turkey: 54 percent of Turks would not want to live next to a family that supports sharia law. Basically, intolerance is common across the board—39 percent of Turks would not want to live next to anyone with religious beliefs different from their own. In addition, 44 percent of Turks believe that restaurants should close down during fasting in the month of Ramadan, and 77 percent of Turks are of the opinion that if religion and science have conflicting positions, religion is always right. Finally, 79 percent of Turks claim that the only true religion is their own.

These cultural polarizations translate directly into the political arena. Those who factor the religious beliefs of political leaders into their electoral decisions have increased from 63 percent in 2006 to 72 percent in 2012; 55 percent of Turks believe that politicians who do not believe in God are unfit to lead, and 51 percent believe that it is beneficial for pious people to be in leadership positions. A full 63 percent of Turks agree that books and publications that attack religion and religious values should be banned.

THE RISE OF MIDDLE-CLASS POLITICS

Even amid the persistence of intolerant attitudes and deepening societal polarization, a new and promising trend is emerging in Turkish political life. Since 2002 Turkey's sound economic policies have allowed more Turks than ever before to share in the country's prosperity and join the ranks of the middle class. This middle-class emergence, midwifed by the ruling AKP, is changing the nature of politics in Turkey as middle-class Turks from all lifestyles and backgrounds buy into the quintessentially middle-class values of liberal democracy. The AKP has perhaps become a victim of its own success.

Reflecting the intolerance that hampers Turkey's political culture, Prime Minister Erdogan has pushed to remake Turkey in his own image: capitalist and conservative, while dismissing opposing views. His government has promoted a socially conservative, family values agenda, encapsulated by his iconic call for each woman to have at least three children. But there are limits to how far the prime minister can go. Prosperous and well educated, the bulk of Turkey (including many conservatives) is not inclined to bend to authoritarian tendencies, even those of the wildly popular prime minister. The country has crossed a threshold—it is too middle class and too diverse to fall under a one-size-fits-all democracy, and a burgeoning civil society is becoming a grassroots check on the AKP's prerogatives.

Turkey's civil society was brutally crippled after the military coup in 1980, which saw the military shut down all NGOs, including labor unions and even chess clubs. These NGOs remained closed for years as per the military's decree, and many withered away as a result. The 1980 coup had followed a decade of political violence in the country between the government and radical right-wing groups on the one hand and radical leftists on the other (the communists also fought among themselves). The violent leftist and right-wing groups were attached to key NGOs, so that even after the military regime ended in 1983 and NGOs were permitted, many Turks shied away from old civil society groups.

The birth of a middle class in the country in the late 1980s and the 1990s allowed new NGOs to form, such as those promoting women's rights. But many of these urban groups failed to appeal to mainline citizens across Anatolia. Turkey's civil society remained weak. When mass demonstrations took place, they failed to bring forth change. In fact, often times these rallies were sponsored by the government, as was the case in 1989 when Turks took to the streets following the government's call to protest discrimination against Turks in Bulgaria. In other cases, demonstrations were limited to specific groups, such as rallies held by Alevis in 1993 to protest the firebombing of a hotel in central Turkey that killed a number of prominent Alevi and leftist artists. In other instances, demonstrations were linked to the military, such as the 2007 rallies in which secularists Turks took to the streets to protest the AKP.

Because this rally was partly a call for the military to put pressure on politicians, it failed to garner widespread legitimacy among the public.

But we may be witnessing a turning point. Turkey's rising middle-class majority has infused Turkish civil society with genuine substance—and Turkey's leaders will ignore this factor at their peril, even when they command clear majorities at the ballot box. During the height of the Gezi protests, Turkish president and former AKP leader Abdullah Gul admitted as much, conceding that the leadership had "gotten the message" that democracy is more than "just winning elections." As a nation, Turkey will need to draw on these positive trends if it is to overcome the various deep-rooted political challenges that loom in the coming years.

7 | Can Turkey Make It?

If increased social in tolerance is one major problem Turkey has to address, the Kurdish issue is another, and nowhere is this challenge more visible than in the southeastern city of Diyarbakir. This is not because Diyarbakir is the world's largest Kurdish city, as it is often touted. That distinction goes to Istanbul, which is not only Turkey's largest city, but also the country's city with the largest Kurdish community, probably around two million Kurds. Diyarbakir, a city on the Tigris River with nearly a million citizens is, however, the center of Kurdish politics in Turkey.

MAKING THE KURDS WELCOME AT HOME

It is hard to say exactly how many Kurds live in Turkey because Turkish censuses do not collect any data on ethnicity. However, recent surveys suggest that as many as 15 percent of the country's citizens could be of ethnic Kurdish origin.[1] The presence of so many Kurds as a non-Turkish ethnicity in the country's population is not so surprising. Turkey is predominantly a multiethnic Muslim nation. In addition to the Muslim Kurds, the country's population also includes a large number of other non-Turkish Muslim ethnicities. For example, around one million Circassians migrated to Turkey in the middle of the nineteenth century when the Russian Tsars expelled them from the northern Caucasus.[2] At that time the Muslim population of Turkey stood at nine million.

Hence, it is likely that the Circassians constitute just around 10 percent of the Turkish population. Yet, despite their relative size, the Circassians and millions of other non-Turkish Ottoman Muslims, from Bosnians to Greek Muslims, have integrated into the Turkish population. Some of the country's Kurds, such as the Alevi Kurds (who mostly share an affinity with the secular Turkish identity) and the millions of Kurds who live in western Turkey have integrated into the country's population, though many others have not. However, the Kurds are unique among all the non-Turkish Muslim groups in Turkey. Not all of them have integrated into the Turkish nation. Whereas none of the other non-Muslim groups espouse a separate national identity, the Kurds do. Why are the Kurds different than the others?

A number of reasons rooted in history could help explain the Kurds' unique alignment vis-à-vis the Turkish nation. Once again, it all goes back to the Ottomans. Turkish nationalism became a potent force in the late Ottoman Empire and also during the early years of the Kemalist republic in the 1920s. The Ottoman Empire broke apart across ethno-religious *millet* lines in the Balkans, where Turkish nationalism also emerged as a potent force in the late nineteenth century. While Balkan Christian nationalisms wanted to expel all Turks and other Muslims from the peninsula, the nascent Turkish nationalists aimed to transform the Ottoman Muslim community into a viable modern force by considering all Ottoman Muslims as members of the prospective Turkish national community, regardless of their ethnic origins. This effort strengthened following the Balkan Wars of 1912–13, in which the Ottomans lost 69 percent of its population and 83 percent of its territory in Europe.[3] Ottoman Muslims in the Balkans had nowhere to go but to Turkey and the embrace of Turkish nationalism.

As the Ottoman Empire crumbled, Turkish nationalism, as a rising ideology, substituted Ottoman Muslim-ness with Turkishness, asking Bosnians, Greek and Bulgarian Muslims, Albanians, and other Ottoman Muslims, such as the Kurds in Turkey to identify themselves as Turks. Ethnicity did not matter. The Turkish nation could become viable only if it included the millions of Ottoman Muslims who lived in the midst of the Turks and shared their fate as the Empire imploded and the Ottoman Muslims in Turkey faced Allied invasion following World War I. This explains why after Ataturk liberated Turkey in 1922, Kemalism, the apogee of Turkish nationalism and secularism, would also ironically consider shared Muslim identity, but not Islamic practice, as the basis of Turkishness.[4]

Surprisingly this late Ottoman-Kemalist stance presented few challenges for the Balkan Muslims, such as Bulgarian Pomak Muslims, as well as other immigrant non-Turkish Muslims, such as the Circassians. These groups had previously been members of the Ottoman Muslim *millet*. Whereas Kemalism viewed the former Muslim *millet* to be the same as the contemporary Turkish nation, this allowed the Circassians, Pomaks, and other Balkan and Caucasus Muslims to make a rather voluntary transition into the Turkish nation.

This was not the case for the Kurds who did not share with the Turks, or for that purpose with Bosnians and Circassians, a strong and ancient memory of having been part of the former Muslim *millet* of the Ottoman Empire. While the vast Ottoman lands extended from Central Europe to the Red Sea, the territories that could be considered Ottoman par excellence are, in fact, more limited. The sultans established their authority and installed classical Ottoman institutions, such as the *millet* system, only in a core group of territories that they captured in the earlier centuries of the empire that stretched from the Danube River in the west to the Black Sea in the north, the Mediterranean in the south, and the Euphrates in the east. As the empire expanded in size in the sixteenth century though, faced with the gargantuan task of running a vast mostly land-based state, the Ottomans decided to manage their newly acquired lands often by leaving such territories under their pre-Ottoman rulers and institutions, demanding only loyalty and taxes from their inhabitants. Therefore, Ottoman identity and institutions did not deeply penetrate territories captured after the fifteenth century, including lands beyond the Euphrates or the Danube, or to North Africa and Arabia.

Enter the Kurds. This group, whose traditional homeland lies east of the Euphrates, outside the core Ottoman territories, was therefore not Ottomanized in the premodern era to the same extent of the non-

Turkish Muslims in the Balkans. Throughout the following Ottoman centuries, Kurdish areas were largely autonomous from Istanbul, and local leaders (*beys*) ruled over these lands that the Ottomans called Kurdistan.[5] To put it succinctly, in the classical Ottoman era a Kurd in what is now southeastern Turkey most likely did not see himself as "Ottoman" in the way that a Slavic Bosnian Muslim in Sarajevo did.

During the nineteenth century the Ottoman Empire centralized, turning into a modern state. Then Istanbul finally brought the peripheral lands, including Kurdistan and Arabia, under its direct rule. The Kurds also became Ottomans, but the empire collapsed not long after that. In the end the Kurds' Ottoman identity was never as deeply rooted as that of the Bosnians or other Balkan Muslims. Hence as Ataturk established modern Turkey out of the ashes of the Ottoman Empire, bringing together lands west of the Euphrates, as well as in the east, compared to other non-Turkish Muslims in Turkey, the Kurds stood in a unique position vis-à-vis Turkish nationalism: they had not been Ottoman enough to become proud Turks now.

Other reasons also complicated the Kurds' voluntary embrace of Turkish nationalism. Various non-Muslim ethnicities lived in Turkey by the time Ataturk turned it into a nation-state in the interwar period.[6] Staunchly laïque (anti-religiously secular in the European fashion), heavily centralized, and proudly nationalist, Ataturk's Turkey resembled contemporary France, the role model and blueprint for statecraft in much of central, southern, and eastern Europe in the late nineteenth and early twentieth centuries. But again the Kurds were different than all other non-Turkish groups in this new Kemalist Turkey: they were the most sizable non-Turkish group in Turkey, comprising more than 10 percent of the country's population in 1920s.

Not just historic identity-related issues but also the present reality hindered the Kurds' voluntary embrace of Turkishness, relative to other non-Turkish Muslims. Various non-Turkish Muslims had been scattered all over Turkey after chaotically arriving in the country as expellees from Russia and Europe. But by the time Ataturk turned the country into a nation-state, the Kurds, who are autochthonous in Anatolia like the Turks, lived clustered and isolated from other Muslims and also from Turks in a contiguous territory in eastern and southeastern Turkey. The Kurds formed the majority of the population in a number of provinces. Non-Turkish immigrant Muslims lived mixed with the Turks west of the Euphrates and married them, and this process also created a physical amalgam: the Turkish nation. The Kurds could not join this amalgam right away because they lived by themselves in rugged, eastern Turkey, which was isolated from the rest of the country: it was not until the late 1930s that railway lines penetrated this area, and then only a few, and not until the 1950s that highways came to the region, again only a few.

Ataturk's secularization and centralization efforts also did not play well with the deeply religious Kurds who also relished a memory of being semi-autonomous under the Ottomans. It is telling in this regard that the single most important uprising against Ataturk's reforms, Sheikh Said uprising of 1925, took place in the Kurdish areas and was led by a religious leader.

A final factor that has complicated the Kurds' passionate embrace of Turkish nationalism is their relative poverty. Much of Turkey was poor until 1980s when then prime minister and later president Turgut Ozal opened the country to the global economy, paving the way for prosperity. While Turkey was poor, eastern Turkey has always been poorer than the rest of the country. The region's destitution is rooted, among other reasons, in the fact that it was destroyed multiple times during and following World War I. Eastern Turkey never fully recovered from the triple burning of some of cities and infrastructure at that time, namely by the Armenian, Ottoman, and Russian armies.[7]

The region's remoteness (it is distant from navigable seas and the rest of the country) and rugged nature (the average altitude in eastern Turkey is 6,500 feet) did not allow it to develop in the 1980s when the rest of the country took off. Accordingly poverty has lasted in this region to this date. Turks too live in eastern Turkey, where they form the majority of the population in the country's equally rugged and cold northeast. While these Turks are as poor as the Kurds in the southeast, their resentment has naturally not become an ethnic one. The Kurds' relative deprivation compared to the rest of the country, though, has

Fig. 2. Diyarbakir Ulu Mosque. Courtesy of Nevit Dilmen.

led to ethnicity-based resentment among them, following the rise of Kurdish nationalism in the late twentieth century. Such resentment, among other reasons, has in return boosted Kurdish nationalism with strong leftist antecedents.

Diyarbakir is a laboratory for observation of this phenomenon. This is the home of BDP, a Kurdish nationalist movement and the fourth largest party in the Turkish legislature. Diyarbakir is the incubator of Kurdish nationalism in the country, and it is a platform for observing how the Kurds are increasingly imagining themselves as a separate nation from the Turks. The ancient city that forms Diyarbakir's core is a typical Fertile Crescent citadel, with three and a half miles of medieval walls surrounding mosques: synagogues; Assyrian, Chaldean, and Armenian churches; stone houses; and arched walkways. In the heart of the old town is the city's central Grand Mosque (Ulu Cami). This is a symbolic building that speaks volumes about southeastern Turkey's historically weak connections to Istanbul. The mosque lacks a central dome but is adorned by an *evantine*. Its architectural style is more red-

Fig. 3. Sultan Ahmed Mosque. Courtesy of Wikimedia Commons.

olent of the Umayyad Mosque in Damascus than the Blue Mosque in Istanbul, which was modeled after the Church of Hagia Sophia, the blueprint for mosque architecture from the Euphrates to the Balkans. Ulu Cami reminds visitors that they are not in the heart of the Ottoman Empire anymore.

The centrifugal forces that have kept Diyarbakir's Kurds away from the heart of the Turkish nation have been compounded in the late twentieth century by fighting between the Turkish government and the PKK. Although Turkey has been militarily able to keep the PKK under check since the organization launched a campaign against Ankara in 1984, incessant fighting since has left an indelible scar on southeastern Turkey and among the Kurds in this region. Together with other factors, instability has prevented the area from taking part in Turkey's opening to the global economy in the 1980s and the economic miracle of the past decade. Today, whereas average disposable income in Istanbul is 14,873 Turkish lira, in the overwhelmingly Kurdish provinces of southeast Anatolia this number drops to 5,418 Turkish lira.[8]

Fighting has alienated many Kurds, too. In the 1980s Turkey responded to the PKK's Kurdish nationalist message by cracking down on its bans of the Kurdish language in courts and for government use, and even in the media.[9] This move has naturally proven counterproductive. Coupled with the PKK's strategy of violence to intimidate the rural Kurdish population in order to build a logistics and recruitment base, this ban on the Kurdish language helped the PKK build a popular base in the 1980s and the 1990s.

In the past decade, Turkey has removed restrictions on the Kurdish language and even started a publicly funded 24 hour Kurdish language TV.[10] Moreover Ankara now facilitates Kurdish language departments in universities, and recently in June 2012, the AKP government decided to allow Kurdish to be taught as an elective course in middle and high schools.[11]

KURDISH NATIONALISM AND THE "FAR SOUTHEAST"

Perhaps all has come a bit too late, though. Turkey appears to have won the upper hand vis-à-vis the PKK, after weathering a spike of PKK attacks that came on the heels of regional instability ushered in by the Arab Spring.[12] More recently the PKK's leader, Abdullah Ocalan, conceded that the PKK's armed struggle should end, and the Kurds should seek to obtain their goals through peaceful means. But even if the PKK may be defeated, Kurdish nationalism is not. This movement has built a lasting appeal, demonstrated by the constant electoral support of 4 to 6 percent that the BDP garners in the Turkish elections. Still, Turkey can find some solace in this dilemma, too. Whereas Turkey's Kurdish population stands at around 15 percent of the country's population, only a third of the country's Kurds (forming around 5 percent of the electorate) seem to be supporting the Kurdish nationalist movement. This is Ankara's opportunity and challenge alike: not a majority, but a fraction of the country's Kurdish population cannot stand the idea of Turkish nationalism and being counted as Turkish. Instead of folding under the rubric of a post-Ottoman, be it non-ethnic, concept of Turkishness, these Kurds would rather be "just Kurds." In southeast Turkey only 23 percent of the population is receptive to being called a Turk.[13] Moreover, that part of the Kurdish population is almost entirely confined to the country's staunchly Kurdish nationalist "far southeast," an area that stretches from Diyarbakir east to Iran and south to Iraq, straddling the Tigris River. A major portion of the voters in the far southeast, also a strong PKK base, voted for BDP in the 2011 elections. In the seven far southeast provinces the BDP attracted 80 percent support in Hakkari, 72 percent in Sirnak, 52 percent in Batman, 43 percent in Siirt, 52 percent in Mardin, 49 percent in Van, and 60 percent in Diyarbakir.[14]

In other words, "Turkey's Kurdish problem" is really "Turkey's Kurdish problem in the far southeast." This is because Kurdish nationalism has either weak or no appeal among Kurds outside of the far southeast. Take, for instance, Bingol, Adiyaman, Gaziantep, and Malatya—all eastern and southeastern Turkish provinces with large Kurdish populations, if not majorities. Candidates supported by the BDP polled merely 24 percent, 6.5 percent, 5 percent, and 1 percent, respectively, in the 2011 elections in these provinces.[15] One reason explaining weak support for the BDP and Kurdish nationalism in this region is that these provinces in the country's interior have been spared the fighting between the PKK and the government. Such fighting has had a radicalizing effect on Kurds in the far southeast, a region that has been open to PKK infiltration from Iraq and Iran due to the mountainous nature of Turkey's borders with both countries, hence rendering it a major theater of violence.

Another reason that explains the weak appeal of BDP and Kurdish nationalism in this region is that religion trumps nationalism in Turkey. Unlike the far southeast, which is almost entirely Sunni Muslim, the provinces of eastern Turkey that cradle the far southeast have mixed Sunnis and Alevis among the Turks and Kurds. Traditionally the majority Sunnis here (including the Kurds) have voted overwhelmingly for right-wing nationalist, Islamist, and conservative parties—an apparent reaction to the presence of the Alevis (including the Kurds), who identify with secularism, the far-left, the left, and the CHP.

Weak support for Kurdish nationalism and the BDP among Kurds outside of the far southeast is even more pronounced in western Turkey, such as in Istanbul, a city of 14 million that has as many as 2 million Kurds. In the 2011 elections BDP received only 5.3 percent of the vote in Istanbul despite an election alliance it entered with socialist and far left Turkish parties, meaning at least a fraction of the BDP's votes in Istanbul are not Kurdish nationalist. Support for the BDP was equally weak in Bursa, Antalya, and Izmir, other Turkish urban centers that have attracted migrants from all over Turkey, including the Kurdish southeast in the past decade. In these towns the BDP polled 1.5, 2, and 4 percent, respectively. Currently about half of Turkey's Kurdish population is estimated to live in western Turkey. Weak support for the BDP and Kurdish nationalism in these areas is a sign that once the Kurds move to western Turkey, many soon integrate enough into the general Turkish population that they start behaving like "other Turks" at the ballot box. In other words the appeal of Kurdish nationalism weakens for the Kurds once they cross to the west of the historic boundary between the core and peripheral areas of the Ottoman Empire, migrating west of the Euphrates River. These Kurds then gradually join Turkey's prosperous, and multiethnic, prima facie Turkish, yet Muslim majority. Kurdish nationalism has little chance to become a potent force in western Turkey.

Hence, solving the Kurdish problem in Turkey is really about addressing the political demands of the approximately 5 million Kurds in the seven far southeast provinces. For these Kurds, Kurdish nationalism is and will remain a powerful force.

Interestingly, in addition to BDP the only other party that does well in the far southeast is the ruling AKP, which received 38 percent of the vote in these seven provinces in the 2011 elections. The AKP's appeal in this region is to the religious and conservative Kurds while the BDP appeals to nonreligious, secularist, and nationalist Kurds. Conservatism versus secularism is a powerful fault line. Take, for instance, the role of women in both parties. Whereas 8 of the 22 BDP MPs from the far

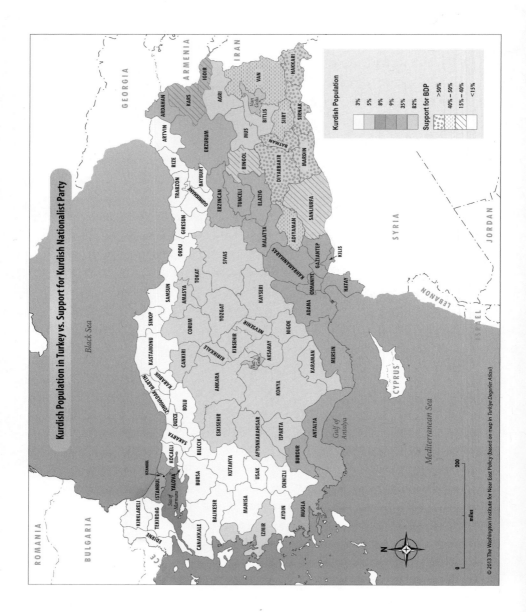

Map 3. Kurdish population in Turkey versus support for Kurdish Nationalist Party.
Courtesy of the Washington Institute for Near East Policy.

southeast in the BDP's parliamentary club are women, there are only 4 women among the 18 AKP deputies representing the seven provinces in the same area.

Kurdish politics in the southeast is shaped by the BDP-AKP fault line. Tellingly, in the 2011 elections the AKP and BDP received over 87.3 percent of the vote in these seven provinces collectively. With the two parties having such different platforms, and the region being split between them, there is almost a political stalemate between the AKP and the BDP in the far southeast. This is a challenge, especially for the governing party at a moment when Turkey is debating writing its first civilian-made constitution. The question is what sort of political rights to grant to the Kurds. The BDP pushes for a maximum amount of group rights, including recognition of the Kurds as a national community and recognition of Kurdish as an official language in the country's constitution and broad autonomy for the Kurdish provinces.[16] The AKP has little to gain politically from writing such promises into Turkey's next charter. Such a stance on the Kurdish issue would win the party few votes among the pro-BDP Kurds in the southeast and would likely cost the AKP support elsewhere in the country, with many Turkish nationalists opposing Turkey's reconfiguration as a binational state of Turks and Kurds. This is especially crucial for Prime Minister Erdogan, who is said to have his eye on Turkey's first popularly elected presidency in 2014.[17] For Erdogan, the presidency is the paramount political prize. Turkey's parliamentary system allocates some powers to the president, while retaining the prime minister as the chief executive. Still, Erdogan likely aspires to the position, arguably since this is the seat where Ataturk sat, and getting there through the ballot box would be an incredible achievement for this politician who has altered Ataturk's laïque legacy. This is where the issue of rights for the Kurds comes in. Erdogan needs at least 50 percent of the Turks to vote for him. His party received 49.9 percent of the vote in the most recent elections, and the Turkish leader believes he cannot afford to lose any support in the run-up to 2014. A liberal stance on the Kurdish issue would not win Erdogan enough Kurdish nationalist votes to offset the many Turkish nationalist votes he would lose; hence the AKP's unwillingness to move forward with more revolutionary rights to the Kurds, though the AKP will continue to press for peace with the PKK in order to prevent terrorism, which hurts the ruling party electorally.

ADDRESSING KURDISH WELTSCHMERZ

Turkey's Kurdish problem will not simply disappear if left to smolder on its own. And due to shifting regional dynamics following the Arab Spring, Turkey is now more pressed than ever to do something to address its Kurdish problem. In 2011 the police arrested thousands of Kurdish nationalists, linked to the Union of Communities in Kurdistan (KCK), a pro-PKK political umbrella. Authorities alleged that the KCK members are working for the benefit of the PKK. Some of these people could be connected to the outlawed and violent PKK. Many others, however, represent the BDP, a legal force in the Turkish legislature that espouses civilian politics, although they refuse to explicitly denounce the PKK.

To make things worse, on December 28, 2011, the Turkish military accidentally targeted a convoy of Kurdish smugglers, mistaking them for PKK members as they crossed the Turkish-Iraqi border. The accident resulted in the death of thirty-four Turkish citizens. This killing could not have come at a worse time. Many nationalist Kurds are especially angry now that Ankara's "2009 Kurdish Opening" was reeled in without meeting the expectations of Kurds in the southeast. At any other time Ankara could have ignored this Kurdish anger, but not today.

Until recently Ankara could have simply told the Turkish Kurds that "they have it really good," given the country's economic boom and political liberalization. Not so long ago, Turkish leaders could have made a convincing case simply by saying, "given the conditions of the Kurds in the adjacent autocratic states, the Kurds should appreciate what they have."

This can no longer be said. For one thing, the Iraqi Kurds now "have it really good" as well, and many Turkish Kurds envy the autonomy enjoyed by their ethnic kin in Erbil and Sulaimaniyah in northern Iraq. The Iraqi Kurds are all but independent, and Turkey's politically active Kurdish community suffers some status anxiety over this fact. There is also economic envy. Until the past decade Diyarbakir and other Kurdish-majority cities in Turkey appeared more prosperous than Sulaimaniyah and Erbil. Today, the opposite could be true.

There is also the fact that Turkish Kurds are now exposed to the Iraqi Kurds and see what the latter have. Ankara's recent rapprochement with the Iraqi Kurds has made the Turkish-Iraqi border a line that exists only on paper.[18] Many Turkish Kurds cross daily into northern Iraq for trading. Some receive education there, and others live together and marry with the Iraqi Kurds, witnessing firsthand the growth of a Kurdish state and pride nearby. The Iraqi Kurds' rise has created *Weltschmerz*, relative pain, among Turkish Kurds, who envy what the Iraqi Kurds have, and they want even more.

Events in Syria compound Ankara's problem by increasing the Turkish Kurds' relativity-based social pain. Ever since the Assad regime's authority started to weaken in Syria during summer 2012, Syrian Kurdish parties and groups have started to take control of some of the country's cities, including Kobani (*Ayn al-Arab*) and Afrin. As the Assad regime contracts, the Kurds are establishing control over their own zones and making demands for constitutional recognition in post-Assad Syria. If they cannot achieve full-fledged autonomy, they will at least have political power and recognition—hence, more *Weltschmerz* for the Turkish Kurds.

With the Iranian Kurds enjoying their own Kurdistan province, even though Iran is far from being a democracy, Turkish Kurds in the near future will go from being the "luckiest Kurds" in the Middle East to nearly the most politically underprivileged Kurds in the region. This is where Turkey's new constitution comes in. If Ankara grasps this opportunity to create a truly liberal charter that broadens everyone's rights, including those of the Kurds, perceptions of injustice relative to Turkey's neighbors will carry less weight.

A NEW SOCIAL CONTRACT

If Turkey is to emerge as a regional power, it needs lasting domestic stability, a development that would allow the country to focus its creative energy outward. Addressing the Kurdish problem, the country's most pressing problem, within the framework of a new constitution might be the best means to this end. So is bringing together the country's two disparate halves by using the same charter as the basis for a social contract that defines liberties for all Turks but also ensures that these liberties cannot be used to trample others' rights.

A new liberal charter would also help bring Turkey's ambitions to serve as a model for countries experiencing the Arab Spring closer to reality. Only by becoming a truly liberal democracy can Turkey hope to present itself as a model to be emulated by Arabs seeking democracy.

Turkey is not the only country with grand designs for its neighborhood. Other regional heavyweights, especially Iran, present competing visions for an emerging order in the Middle East. At home the old balances that kept these relations stable are history and a new modus vivendi between Islamists and secularists, conservatives and liberals, has yet to take solid form.

To that end the AKP must realize that secular, liberal Turkey, which comprises around half of the country's population, is too big to ignore. (And the secular liberals must realize that, unlike a decade ago, Turkey has a large, established conservative-Islamist elite and political party with widespread support). Both halves of the country must work together toward a new constitution, lest Turkey suffer a split down the middle. In this regard the June 2013 protests that brought Istanbul to a standstill for over two weeks are a case in point. Further paralysis would be bad for the country—the only experiment in the world that unites Islam and democracy—and for those watching it.

Today Turkey is a very different country than it was in 2002 when the AKP came to power. Back then the party, rooted in political Islam, represented a counterforce to challenge the secular parties that had long governed the country. The AKP also had a message of moderation, abandoning Islamism and instead moving toward the center. At this time the party embraced the EU accession process and pushed for liberalizing reforms that included rights for Kurds. These moves helped build a rainbow coalition of supporters around the AKP, ranging from Kurdish nationalists to large businesses, liberals, and Islamist-conservatives.

Ten years later the AKP is no longer the political underdog. After ruling for almost a decade, the AKP has become the establishment par excellence. Unlike in the late 1990s, the pro-AKP groups now dominate large parts of the Turkish media, academia, business world, and airwaves. At the same time, though, popular support has perhaps become the Achilles' heel of the AKP's success. Moderation brought the AKP popularity. Yet the more popular it became, the more the AKP felt it could ignore centrist consensual politics and the liberal vision for EU membership. In due course the party abandoned the EU process and instead started to go after those who disagree with it, including independent media and the courts. For example, according to a 2012 report from the international advocacy group the Committee to Protect Journalists, with forty-nine journalists in jail, Turkey is the country with the highest number of journalists in prison—more than either China or Iran.[19]

Furthermore, after amending the country's constitution in 2010, the AKP now single-handedly appoints a majority of the high court without a confirmation process. Large businesses are disheartened by heavy-handed treatment of secular companies by the AKP, who attempt to force these secular businesses to toe the party line. In a recent case the AKP slapped Dogan Media Group—the country's biggest media conglomerate—with a record $3.5 billion fine, which, combined with an earlier fine of $500 million, exceeded Dogan's net worth.

The AKP can technically draft and adopt Turkey's new constitution. And if it is to become a first-rate society, rising as regional power and presenting itself as a source of inspiration for Arab societies, Turkey needs its first civilian constitution. Nonetheless, a made-by-AKP constitution will lack legitimacy in the eyes of half of the country, including large businesses, Kurdish nationalists, and liberal and secularist Turks, just as a constitution made only by the liberal Turks would lack legitimacy in the eyes of AKP supporters.

The key is for both sides to realize that neither owns Turkey, for the AKP and non-AKP halves of Turkey are equally large in size and importance. Secular and liberal Turks have to adjust to this reality; unlike a decade ago Turkey now has a large, established conservative elite and a political party supported by many people. None of this will simply disappear.

By the same token, though, the AKP has to realize that secular liberal Turkey, incorporating around half of the country's population and many of its large businesses, is too big for the AKP to take over and digest or just ignore. Reality necessitates that both halves of the country work together toward a new constitution lest Turkey split, potentially violently, in the middle.

Setting Turkish society on the right course will be easier said than done, for it requires not only replacing an illiberal constitutional text but, more importantly, hitting the reset button on a habit that has inflamed the political atmosphere for decades: the tendency to see politics as extending into every detail of daily life. Liberals in Turkey have tied their hopes to the promise that Turkey's new rulers will use their historic opportunity to make Turkey a place where people from every walk of life can enjoy equal freedom to express themselves, no matter their religion, lifestyle preference, ethnicity, or political persuasion. Yet the instinct to deny diversity remains. For example, Prime Minister Erdogan has opposed granting Alevi places of worship the same state subsidies granted to Sunni mosques, and in May 2012, Turkey's women were suddenly confronted with a bill to effectively outlaw abortion after Erdogan proclaimed that abortion was tantamount to murder.[20] Liberal concerns arose again when world-famous Turkish pianist Fazil Say was hauled to court in October 2012 over Twitter comments he made insulting Islamists.[21] On the Kurdish issue the AKP's reforms have been paired with set-backs, such as the imprisonment of Busra Ersanli, a professor who was held in prison for over eight months for lectures she gave to members of the Kurdish nationalist BDP.

Sooner or later the opposing camps in Turkey must recognize diversity is not going to disappear. A new social contract could underline this simple fact, acting as the best panacea for increasing social intolerance in Turkey. As the social power of religious conservatives rises, and Turkey's secularists dig in their heels, the most mundane topics in politics and daily life are becoming bitterly contested battlegrounds. Changing the way these issues are framed will be the defining challenge for Turkey's political future, and one that will require truly high-minded leadership on the part of the AKP.

AND THE SECULARISTS' SHARE: NEW KEMALISM

Turkey's twentieth-century experience with Kemalism—a Europe-oriented top-down Westernization model—has largely come to an end. Hard as it might be, secularist Turks need to understand and accept this fact. While Kemalism may be dead, Kemalists are alive in Turkey, dominating parts of the country, including cities such as Izmir, the country's third largest city. Turkish secularists who oppose any manifestation of religion in the public sphere have watched the AKP's rise with deep suspicion. Yet, it is time for them to come to terms with new Turkey, for the AKP and the other half of Turkey that supports that party's platform will simply not go away.

Can the CHP, Turkey's main opposition movement and the heir of Mustafa Kemal Ataturk's legacy of a Western and secular Turkey, challenge the governing AKP in the upcoming 2014 elections and later? Ever since coming to power in 2002, the AKP has successfully injected social conservatism into the country's social life and has done so with growing popular support.

So, can the CHP hope to defeat the AKP at the ballot box? Until recently, the answer was no, for the outdated and fatigued CHP was unable to put forth a convincing vision of how Turkey should evolve that could oppose the AKP's dynamic model.

But now things are different: in May 2010 the CHP elected the new and charismatic leader Kemal Kilicdaroglu. Kilicdaroglu then managed to win enough support from CHP delegates to form a new party assembly composed of fresh faces, including a twenty-six-year-old woman with a PhD, diplomats from Turkey's pro-Western Foreign Ministry, as well as businesswomen, union leaders, liberal college professors, and economists. Despite earlier predictions the old CHP guard would prevent Kilicdaroglu from having his vision of a "New Kemalism"—a liberal and updated version of modern Turkey's founding ideology—elected to the party assembly, Kilicdaroglu has succeeded in changing the CHP's top echelons.

Since Turkish political parties are top-down structures, this means the CHP will now change from the top down. And in the run-up to the 2011 elections, the AKP faced a real challenge from a renewed opposition for the first time since 2002. Unlike its previous challenger, the new CHP ran on a platform that was forward looking, with a vision to create a new, liberal and pro-Western Turkey. Although hopes run high, it is still unclear if the CHP will ever truly become a fully liberal force, able to challenge the AKP. The CHP's base is deeply divided between those who have accepted the realities of the new Turkey and those who are determined to struggle blindly against them even if it means becoming increasingly marginalized. This has made managing the party a vexing task for Kilicdaroglu, who has demonstrated an imperfect record when it comes to crafting a coherent and constructive message.

Ever since the AKP assumed power, analysts had been worried by two interrelated problems in the Turkish political system: first, an increasingly authoritarian ruling party that tramples over democratic checks and balances (for instance, punishing independent media with tax fines); and second, an ineffective opposition unable to define its vision of where Turkey should go if not along the AKP path.

If the CHP can consolidate, it could be in a position to compete against the AKP's model of a socially conservative society in which religiosity is a growing source of political legitimacy.

A fact that is missing to most observers of politics in Muslim countries—and in fact to most Muslims and Turks—is that conservatism and religiosity are not conjoined twins. One can be religious and not conservative, or conservative but not religious. Yet the AKP defines the two as interchangeable in the Turkish context. Take for instance, the story of a young woman in Istanbul of mixed Muslim–Greek Orthodox heritage. This woman told me she had applied for a job with a branch of the AKP-controlled Istanbul municipality. At her job interview the woman was told the AKP government would hire her if she agreed to wear an Islamic-style headscarf. When she responded that she was also

Greek Orthodox, she was told, "You don't need to convert; all you have to do is cover your head."

This exhibits just how the AKP is successfully combining religiosity with social conservatism. And through this strategy the party is gaining legitimacy in a mostly religious society while driving conservatism across the board. In order to challenge this strategy and set up a serious alternative to the AKP in the polls, the CHP must de-couple social conservatism from religiosity and thus end the AKP's monopoly over the "the party of religion" brand.

This way Kilicdaroglu's New Kemalism could uphold the separation of religion and government, while taking advantage of the distinction between social conservatism and religiosity. Turks are by definition a religious people; opinion polls show that over 90 percent of Turks believe in God.[22] The CHP has to make peace with this fact and adjust its vision of secularism to accommodate religious practice. Yet, at the same time, New Kemalism ought to be clear on social conservatism. While there is nothing wrong with social conservatism per se, when imposed by a government—as demonstrated by the experience of the aforementioned Muslim–Greek Orthodox woman—it is incompatible with the idea of liberal Western society that New Kemalism would wish to represent.

In other words, the CHP has to reinvent itself as the party of liberalism in order to find a place where it can be at peace with religion but also promote socially liberal values. Then Kilicdaroglu not only would be in a position to challenge the AKP but would also bask in the glory of achieving a first, unhitching religiosity and social conservatism. With this, Kilicdaroglu's New Kemalism would also open the path for a liberal-religious polity in a predominantly Muslim society. This is indeed a tall order, but it is the only way the CHP can hope to challenge the AKP in the ballot box.

ECONOMIC STABILITY AND LIBERAL DEMOCRACY

A consensus on liberal democracy between the government and the opposition is a sine qua non for Turkey's potential rise as a global power.

So is the governing party's ability to foster stable conditions for economic growth, which served as the engine for Turkey's rising profile abroad. Credited with setting this new dynamic in motion, the AKP was rewarded with unprecedented electoral success, not only solidifying their own power but also giving them the tools to further promote political stability. Thanks to this virtuous cycle, Turkish confidence is at an all-time high, spurring Ankara to look to raise its profile, not only in its region but also globally, as witnessed by Turkey's bids to host the G20, the 2020 World Expo, and Olympic Games, as well as it 2014 ascendance to the IMF executive directorship. The result is a new Turkey with influence that spans multiple continents.

The AKP is working hard to consolidate the domestic conditions that have been key to Turkey's rise. Yet some of Turkey's toughest domestic challenges still lie ahead. Perhaps the most difficult challenge will be reforming Turkey's deeply ingrained social and political culture that has stifled pluralism and stoked conflict in the past. To this end the AKP continues to take bold steps. Most recently reports surfaced that Turkey is considering reopening the Halki Greek Orthodox seminary that was shut down in 1971 when the Cyprus issue blew up. Reinstituting this Christian school, the only Orthodox seminary in the country, would eliminate one area of discrimination against Turkish Christians and, more importantly, would open the debate on a bigger issue: it is time Turkey grew into a society of consensual politics, one that brings together the country's small and large disparate halves, from its Kurds to its Christians, its Jews to its Alevis. This would also mean establishing a well-ordered political framework to lend inclusiveness and coherence to Turkey's fragmented political landscape that includes nationalists, secularists, religious conservatives, liberals, socialists, and minority rights activists.

ENDING THE KULTURKAMPF

The most visible activity in this direction is the AKP-led initiative for constitutional reform. Turkey has had five constitutions so far, including Ottoman-era ones, but it has shared the same distain for public inclusion in their crafting. The current constitution is perhaps the most illiberal of all. It has three articles that state Kemalism is Turkey's official ideology, Turkish is its national language, and Turkishness is the basis of country's citizenship. The charter adds that these articles cannot be scrapped or amended. The AKP is intent on making an entirely new constitution, but it seems reluctant to alter these three articles. The big picture is that this is an opportunity Turkey cannot miss if it is truly determined to become the first Muslim majority society to practice a fully mature liberal democracy. In this regard Turkey can learn lessons in ending its *Kulturkampf* from countries such as Spain, which emerged from its own *Kulturkampf*, deeper than Turkey's, in the 1970s to evolve into a true liberal democracy. Turkey can and should draw a radically liberal charter that makes it unconstitutional to discriminate against someone due to their religion, language, gender, ethnicity, sexual orientation, political affiliation, ideology, and religious practice or lack thereof. This would be the best way for Turkey to create breathing space for its disparate and fighting halves while providing a truly inspirational document for the Arab Spring countries. Sealing this fundamental social accord will set the stage for Turkey to unleash the creative energy of its diverse cultural richness and allow the nation to focus its energies outward to accomplish its regional and global ambitions.

A PATH TO FOLLOW: ISTANBUL'S REEMERGING COSMOPOLITANISM

One forward path for Turkey is taking lessons from Istanbul's reemergent cosmopolitanism. Istanbul is a living example of the success of liberalism and should serve as a comfort for the Turks unsure about liberal democracy that this is the only way forward. After the Ottoman Empire collapsed in the nineteenth century, modern Turkey was born of its ashes. Led by Ataturk, Turkey became a new state dominated by an elite who sought to sever all ties with their Ottoman past. Multiculturalism swiftly ended; Italians, Russians, Greeks, and Armenians left the city, and Istanbul became almost entirely Muslim and Turkish. The city's imperial luster seemed to be lost forever.

Lately, however, this trend of homogenization has been reversed.

Economic growth has driven this process. In the past decade the country's economy has nearly tripled in size, experiencing the longest spurt of prosperity in modern Turkish history. With thirty-five billionaires in 2012, Turkey already boasts more uber-wealthy citizens today than Japan, Canada, or Italy.[23] Turkey is the only growing and stable country in its region. Hence, many Eastern Europeans, such as Romanians, Moldovans, and Russians, are returning to the city, looking for trade and jobs. Azerbaijani, Ukrainian, and Kazakh billionaires are coming to Istanbul to find a safe haven for the wealth they have amassed in the energy and metals trades.

Initially attracted by the international trade and finance opportunities Istanbul offered, Western Europeans also returned. Some of them eventually settled down and intermarried with the Turks, a convergence reminiscent of the economic boom years that graced the Ottoman Empire.

Even Armenians are coming back, thanks to economic growth. Since the collapse of the Soviet Union, tens of thousands of Armenian citizens have arrived in Istanbul in search of jobs. This influx has been so significant that Armenians now outnumber the city's 60,000-strong Turkish Armenian community. Responding to the influx, Ankara recently expanded its laws to allow the children of undocumented Armenian immigrants access to the Turkish school system. The return of Armenians "has reached a meaningful point," says Aram Atesyan, acting patriarch of the Armenian Church in Turkey.

The Greeks are coming back, too. The financial crisis in Greece has started a mass migration of professionals to "Constantinople," including academics, doctors, and teachers. Take Georgia Kapoutsi, for instance, a twenty-nine-year-old English teacher from Athens who recently moved to Istanbul to "learn, work and live." "Wealthier Greeks are returning to the city for its quality of life and to escape Greece's chaos," she notes. Istanbul's trendy Cihangir and Beyoglu neighborhoods are brimming with wealthy Athenians who fill the district's humming bistros and vintage stores.

Istanbul's re-emerging cosmopolitan identity sweeps even wider than the original Ottoman realm. Filipinos, for example, are coming to Istanbul as babysitters, and Chinese have built the city's first Chinatown in downtown Taksim. Taner Akpinar, a Turkish specialist in labor economics, points out that "due to free labor movements, Istanbul has been a haven for immigrants from the Asian countries." For instance, whereas only a decade ago central Anatolian Turks and Kurds from eastern Turkey provided domestic help in upper-class households, now rich Istanbulites are increasingly hiring East Asians, looking beyond traditional Ottoman realms. Indeed, Istanbul is opening to a whole new world.

Subsequently new trends have recently emerged that help restore Istanbul's imperial identity on the one hand, while challenging Kemalism's nation-state ethos on the other. Istanbul provides lessons to the Turks that they should have nothing to fear from becoming a multicultural society again.

CAPTURING ITS KURDISH MOMENT IN SYRIA AND BEYOND

Another fear Turkey needs to overcome is that of Kurdistan.[24] This is especially important since the Arab Spring has presented Turkey with a rare opportunity, its own Kurdish moment.

As Syria's civil war deepens, the specter has arisen of escalating armed hostility between Syria and Turkey, once a friend of the Assad regime. Whereas a century ago it was Western powers that dismantled and carved up the Ottoman Empire after World War I, today Turkey can place itself in the driver's seat of shaping the borders of the emerging Near East map.

Syria's slide into ungovernability suggests that unlike in Libya at the moment, splintering and partition are increasingly likely options, unless the Assad regime falls precipitously. During early stages of the conflict, ironically, many spoke of a Lebanon model for its larger imposing patron Syria—meaning a loose and tenuous confederation of sectarian interests, something of a Bosnia for the Near East. If the conflict in Syria continues unabated, leading to full-blown sectarian war between Alawites and Sunnis and violent ethnic tensions between Arabs and Kurds, the scenario that is more likely to unfold now is more along the Iraq model of de facto zones of semi-independent control: Aleppo and Damascus would still likely be together, though they would be pulled in different directions thanks to countervailing trade links, with Aleppo gravitating north toward its historic hinterland in Turkey and Damascus pivoting for its port in Beirut, Lebanon. There would be a middling Druze enclave in the south. The Kurdish northeast would turn to Iraqi Kurdistan and toward Turkey—the Syrian Kurds would value Ankara as a balancing force against Arab nationalism, a lesson they would fast learn from the Iraqi Kurds, who have made Turkey their protector against Baghdad since 2010. And Alawites would retreat to their traditional stronghold around the Mediterranean port of Latakia.

Regional trends would pull Syria's parts further apart: the more parties vying for sovereignty, the clearer it becomes that the country's partition is already well underway. The timeline by which nominally autonomous zones achieve full sovereignty will surely vary. Iraq's Kurdistan Regional Government (KRG) has remained relatively quiet since the early 1990s after the U.S.-led invasion of Iraq and creation of no-fly zones, but it still remains content as part of Iraq in order to benefit from oil revenues and holding high political offices such as the presidency.

It was between 1915 and the 1920 Treaty of Sevres that Western powers began plotting the partition of the Ottoman Empire, with the Paris Peace Conference of 1919 and the 1923 Treaty of Lausanne all bearing on the various territorial partitions and concessions that were in some cases settled only much later with the British taking over, and dissolving, the French mandates in the Levant after World War II.

This time around, Turkey is NATO's tip of the spear in the region, though NATO's Western leaders are in reaction mode to Syria's collapse. Moreover, Turkey increasingly thinks that Iran is running a Shiite-axis to its south, stretching from Baghdad to the Assad regime to Hezbollah in Lebanon. How should Turkey respond to this once-in-a-century opportunity?

Whereas Turkey has traditionally been hostile to an independent Kurdistan state or entity, the prospect of chronically unstable Sunni Arab neighbors, and the need to counter Iran's Shiite axis, could change this calculus.

The cross-border shelling across the Turkish-Syrian border presents an important case for why Turkey might be better served by buffer states such as Kurdistan and the "Hanseatic city of Aleppo," rather than the far less defined ground realities today.

Somewhere between 10 and 20 percent of the Syrian population is Kurdish, creating a strong case for a greater Kurdish zone of control and eventual autonomy together with fraternal allies in Iraq, particularly given that the largest concentrations of Kurds in Syria live in the north along the Turkish border areas stretching eastward toward Iraq. There is also linguistic commonality among the Turkish, Syrian, and Iraqi Kurds in that zone. These Kurds speak the Kurmanchi variety of Kurdish, as opposed to Iranians and northeastern Iraqi Kurds, who speak the Sorani variety of Kurdish, which is as different from Kurmanchi as Portuguese is from Spanish.

Assad's regime turned a blind eye to PKK activity around Aleppo on its territory last year to preempt a Turkish invasion of the country's rebellious northwestern provinces outside of Aleppo. With his authority collapsing most rapidly in northwestern Syria, Assad now appears powerless to prevent PKK usage of Syrian territory to regroup; thus Turkey ought to favor a new Aleppo-based government that seeks stability and order on its territory and that would act more responsibly, as Iraq's KRG has, in reigning in PKK militias in northern Iraq. Indeed, Kurdish self-defense forces from Syria are now receiving training from Peshmerga forces in Iraqi Kurdistan.

Irrespective of the role of the PKK, Syria's main Kurdish political faction, the PYD, a PKK affiliate, has learned from watching neighboring Iraq and knows that the Sunni power scramble in Damascus following Assad's fall will be united in one respect: putting down Kurdish self-governance ambitions.

Importantly, the Kurds cling to secularism more than Sunni Arabs in the region, so whereas the Kurdish dilemma is a political one for Turkey, it at least lacks the radical religious dimension. Moreover, ethnic Kurds hold prominent positions in the Ankara government. This will help ease in a Syrian Kurdish-Turkish rapprochement, as it has between Ankara and Erbil.

Furthermore, as has been the case with Iraqi Kurdistan, Turkish infrastructure companies have been among the prime beneficiaries of the region's investment boom, winning major contracts for road and airport construction. Turkey is the necessary outlet for Kurdistan's energy resources and a necessary trade partner for any landlocked entity emerging in the post-Syrian aftermath. Turkey's other competitive advantage in Iraq, an advanced economy that lies just next door, will be its advantage also in post-Assad Syria.

All of that does not suggest a rosy path for Ankara. In this regard there are lessons for the Syrian Kurds from Iraqi KRG. In recent years Ankara's policy with the Iraqi Kurds has evolved from open hostility in 2003, when the Iraqi Kurds built their Kurdistan, to open friendship today. As soon as the Iraqi Kurds showed good will on the PKK issue, Ankara reciprocated, building good ties with the Iraqi Kurdistan Regional Government in Erbil. Today Turkey has a diplomatic mission in Erbil, and Turkish Airlines, the country's national flag carrier, flies directly from Erbil not only to Istanbul but also to Antalya, carrying Kurdish vacationers to the Turkish Riviera. And trade between Turkey and the Iraqi Kurds has boomed to such an extent that if Iraqi Kurdistan were an independent country today, Turkey would be its largest trading partner.

Could Turkey deal with the second Kurdistan with the same ease it has learned to deal with the first? Turkey's peace talks with the PKK could contribute toward this end, as the PKK has significant influence among the Syrian Kurds. Turkey has a second challenge if it is to grasp its Kurdish moment. As Ankara makes good friends with the Iraqi Kurds and hopefully also the Syrian Kurds, it has to keep its own disgruntled Kurds happy. Rising Kurdish nationalism across the region has excited the country's Kurds, and Turkey has witnessed a rise in PKK attacks recently, with the group even launching a brazen, if aborted, fall campaign to take over towns in the country's southeast. Politically Ankara's 2009 failed attempt to provide more cultural rights for the country's Kurds has added to the Turkish Kurds' frustrations. Such sentiments will be voiced prominently in the country's 2014 local elections when Kurdish nationalist BDP takes control of cities in southeastern Turkey.

It will be hard for Turkey to maintain leverage over the Syrian and Iraqi Kurds when Turkish Kurds are locked in a struggle against Ankara. As it vies for influence in Syria and Iraq, Ankara has to make peace with its Kurdish community. Lately some Kurdish nationalists are suggesting that this is the Kurds' moment in history. The Kurds may indeed turn the Middle East's post–World War I alignment on its head, but they cannot do this without Turkey. This is in fact Turkey's Kurdish and Middle East moment—if Ankara gets its hand right at home.

8 | Is There Room for Turkey in the West?

Assuming that the new Turkey makes it as a regional force, and a global power, is there room for this new Turkey in the West? More bluntly, does this new Turkey even want to be in the West? The short answer to this question is yes, but not in the way Mustafa Kemal Ataturk or Turgut Ozal, Turkey's liberalizing president during the 1980s, imagined things. Both Ataturk and Ozal saw Turkey as a Western country, period. Ataturk envisioned a strictly secular and nationalist European society in line with fin de siècle thinking. Ozal, on the other hand, a conservative and practicing Muslim, envisioned a Muslim society that was also an integral part of the West and a good friend of the United States. Indeed, Ozal rejuvenated Ankara's dormant EU accession process in 1987 by resubmitting Turkey's membership application (the original application dating back to 1959 had been nearly forgotten by that time). Ozal even stood with Washington after Saddam Hussein invaded Kuwait, closing its major oil pipeline with Iraq to comply with UN sanctions and amassing troops on the border.

This is not the AKP's vision for Turkey. For the country's new leaders Turkey's Muslim and Western identities are mutually exclusive. This is an especially interesting difference given that Ozal and Erdogan are both known to be pious and practicing Muslims. Whereas Ozal believed it was his mission to make Turkey an integral part of the West, Erdogan and his foreign minister Davutoglu envision making Turkey a key leader in the Muslim world's dealings with the West. This vision has resulted in Turkey's autarchic foreign policy in the last decade, also dubbed "strategic depth." That view has occasionally led to in foreign policy rifts between Ankara and Washington on a number of issues, including the 2010 vote at the UN Security Council to call for international sanctions against Tehran's nuclear project. Ankara's vote against the sanctions is indicative of where Turkey's new leaders were tempted to believe that the country belongs: separate from Washington. But more recently the tumult of the Arab Spring and competition against Tehran in Syria and Iraq have led Ankara to revise its erstwhile autarchic foreign policy, and Turkey now seeks security with NATO—a shift symbolized by Ankara's agreement in September 2011 to host a major missile-defense project that is aimed to defend Alliance members against Iranian nuclear weapons.

Still, Turkey's transformation under the AKP and the country's economic move away from Europe appear to have left an indelible mark on the national psyche in terms of Turkey's Western identity. The German Marshall Fund's Transatlantic Trends surveys have documented the extent to which Turkish views have diverged from the West. In 2004, 73 percent of Turks believed membership in the EU would be beneficial, but those numbers had dropped to 38 percent by 2010. The majority of Turks (53 percent) found NATO essential in 2004, but by 2012 this has eroded to 38 percent. In 2010, a notable year for Turkish-European friction, a full 48 percent of Turks felt Turkey had such different values from the West so as to make it non-Western. Moreover, in 2012, 46 percent felt that Asia was more important for Turkey's national interests than the United States, and only 29 percent held the opposing view.[1]

All this is not without consequences for Turkey's foreign policy. According to the same report, in 2010 whereas only 13 percent of Turks desired cooperation with the EU (down from 22 percent in 2009), the percentage of those desiring cooperation with Turkey's Muslim Middle Eastern neighbors had risen to 20 percent, up ten points since 2009. That, in return, has spelled trouble for Turkey's EU vocation, a key test of the country's Western bonds.

Turkey's EU path has always been a very slow and arduous process. Ankara applied to join what is now the EU in 1959, and in 1963 an association agreement came into effect, binding the two together in the political equivalent of "going steady," with both sides agreeing that "one day" Ankara would become a member. This "one day" almost became a reality in the 1970s, when the European community gave Ankara an opening to begin negotiating for accession. At the time, however, Ankara was under its first, and so far only, left-wing government, which castigated the union as a "capitalist club" and rejected the membership offer.[2]

After that Turkey's EU train hit multiple roadblocks, and yet each time Europe and Turkey reset ties, creatively resuscitating Ankara's EU hopes. In 1987, for instance, Ozal decided that the only way to reset Turkey's stalled accession process was to resubmit its 1959 application. Today, as a result, Turkey holds the distinction of being the only country that has submitted two applications for EU membership, both in good standing.

In the 1990s the process withered away again, but true to the nature of their committed relationship, Turkey and the union reset their ties: in 1999 Brussels agreed to consider Ankara's candidacy, demanding political reforms in return. When Turkey finally opened accession talks after completing the reforms in 2005, it seemed as if the accession process would move forward, for a change.

On October 10, 2012, however, the EU issued its progress report, evaluating Ankara's preparations for joining the union. The report is the harshest review that the union has issued on Turkey. Among others things, Brussels criticized the political winds in Turkey, lamenting that "oversight of the executive continues to be hampered by the persistent lack of dialogue and spirit of compromise among political parties." Brussels added that Turkey's trials against alleged coup plotters had become a missed opportunity, "overshadowed by real concerns about their wide scope and the shortcomings in judicial proceedings."[3] Yet rather than serve as a wake-up call for Turkish authorities, the report was either dismissed or outright ridiculed. An AKP deputy with a leadership role in the party's constitutional reform project went on live television to denounce the report by theatrically throwing it into the garbage, and the minister of economy brushed off the report, saying that Turkey's exclusion from the union was really Europe's loss.

Turkey reformed aggressively until it became a candidate country for EU accession in 2005 but dropped the ball after that. When the AKP came to power in 2002, many were satisfied with the party's assurance that it would make EU accession the chief foreign policy goal, despite the party's Islamist pedigree. The promise of a European Turkey helped assuage fears within both Turkey and Europe about the AKP's Islamist roots: if the AKP desired a European Turkey, it could not possibly harbor Islamist tendencies.

Initially the AKP held true to its promise and pushed for EU membership, legislating reforms and making Turkey a candidate country for talks in 2005. However, just as Turkey began accession talks, the party turned its attention to the Middle East, suggesting it would make Turkey a "center country," a bridge earning the trust of both Europe and the Muslim world.

Besides, prior to the election of François Hollande to the French presidency in 2012, vehement French objections significantly undermined Turkey's EU accession prospects and provided Ankara an easy excuse for dragging its feet on reforms. So far, all twenty-three countries (including Norway, which ultimately decided not to join the union) that negotiated for EU membership were ultimately offered accession. Yet from the beginning, Paris treated Turkey differently, opposing membership regardless of the status of current accession talks. Previously accession countries had to complete membership negotiations in one round. In 2005, however, on Paris's insistence, and with backroom support from Berlin, the EU divided the accession materials into thirty-five chapters, creating thirty-five rounds of talks with Ankara as a result. Moreover, the union stipulated that the consent of all twenty-seven member states would be needed for each of these chapters to be opened and closed. So, thirty-five rounds, multiplied by two opening and closing steps, times twenty-seven members means that Turkey had to overcome 1,890 possible vetoes to become a member. Is it any surprise that accession talks are dead? So far, Turkey has completed only the chapter on science and technology, which it closed in 2006. Since then more than a dozen additional chapters have been opened for negotiation, but political disagreement over Cyprus has frozen progress.

Meanwhile, having ingratiated itself to both Brussels bureaucrats and liberal Turks until 2005, the AKP abruptly dropped the EU process just as it was expected to implement the toughest reforms toward full membership. This sudden change was consistent with the AKP's apparent tactical view of EU membership; the party pursued accession as long as it had little domestic cost and garnered the AKP international legitimacy as a pro-EU (and ostensibly non-Islamist) party. However, once substantive accession talks began in 2005 and the domestic economic and political costs of reforms became apparent, the AKP balked, judging the benefits of a cool attitude toward the EU to supersede those of membership in it.

In addition to the AKP's calculations of the domestic political costs of enacting the unpopular reforms, the party's appetite for Europe waned due to the European Court of Human Rights' 2005 decision to uphold Turkey's ban on Islamic-style headscarves on college campuses. The AKP had hoped that Europe would help it recalibrate Turkey's powerful secular norms by making different manifestations of political Islam more permissible. The court's decision suggested, however, that Europe was as content with Turkish secularism *à la Europe* in Turkey. The AKP's loss of interest in the EU was made clear when the party declared 2005 the "Year of Africa," opting to turn the country's attention to a different continent at a rather inopportune time.

In due course the AKP mostly dropped the reform process, allowing the state of reforms to deteriorate. This has meant a move away from liberal values: Turkey dropped twenty spots in the Reporters Without Borders Press Freedom Index, from 102nd out of 175 countries in 2008 to 122nd in 2011.

This impasse has softened somewhat under French president Nicolas Sarkozy's successor, François Hollande. Paris has supported opening negotiating chapters, at the very least allowing the sides to nurture the perception that progress is being made on talks. Germany's chancellor Angela Merkel has also displayed a more nuanced attitude toward Turkey. However, her center right coalition is unlikely to budge on its belief that Turkey is culturally mismatched for the community of European nations.[4] Against these immovable roadblocks the process has come to a standstill. Turkey and the EU have been flirting for five decades now without committing to one another. It seems that for a variety of economic and political reasons both sides like to talk to one another, engaging in "political dating." In the end, though, one or the other gets cold feet, rejecting "political marriage": full membership. This time-tested modus vivendi will characterize future trends, as well.

TURKEY'S STRESS TESTS

This time, though, the relationship will have a new set of parameters. In the past Turkey appeared to need the EU more than the Union needed Turkey. Today the opposite holds true. For starters, Turkey's booming economy stands in stark contrast to the EU's stagnant one. In addition, whereas Turkey has historically seen EU membership as its only political anchor, Ankara feels less compelled to put all its foreign policy eggs into the EU's basket now that it has become a major political actor in the Middle East.

However, the June 2013 protests showed that Turkey still has to improve its democracy, including stronger recognition for freedom of assembly, association, media, and expression. To that end, the EU accession process serves as a soft power anchor: Turkey could make faster progress on freedoms if the EU process were linked to the genuine prospect of eventual entry. This suggests that whereas a decade ago Turkey needed the EU for mostly economic reasons, now the EU is essential to Turkey as an impetus for political advancement. This begs the question, what if Turkey's EU accession talks fail to move? Membership talks have come to such a grinding halt that the proverbial Turkish-EU accession train recalls a joke about the trains in Brezhnev's Soviet Union: with Russia stagnating, the trains did not move and the scenery did not change, so the people said "choo-choo" to delude themselves into thinking they were going somewhere. Like the Russian train passengers, at some point the Turks will realize that their EU train is not moving forward, and they will disembark. This is bad news for the consolidation of liberal democracy in Turkey, as well as for the country's rise in the Middle East as a leader of democracy in the region. So given its particularities, just where is Turkey headed in regard to its relations with the West? Much will depend on how its leaders navigate the challenges ahead. Indeed, a number of "stress tests" await Turkey in the near term.

Liberal Democracy

Turkey is not perfect. But this should not be Europe's argument against Turkey's EU membership. Instead of shutting its doors to Turkey on essentialist grounds, arguing that "Turkey is Muslim and therefore cannot be European," the continent should frame its expectations from Ankara with a European mindset. The EU should expect from Turkey what one expects from any liberal European democracy. A Danish diplomat friend once said, "Turkey is in good shape, because its Islamists would be democrats in Afghanistan." True, but while Turkey's population is predominantly Muslim, like Egypt and other Middle Eastern countries, its political system is a secular democracy like Europe's, and Turkey is an aspiring EU member. Comparing Turkey politically to Muslim Afghanistan would be nearly as inappropriate as comparing the United States to Christian, yet undemocratic Belarus. As Turkey goes soul-searching for what it means to be a liberal, secular democracy, the political yardstick for Turkey should be Italy and France—not Afghanistan and Saudi Arabia.

The Cyprus Issue

In Cyprus a decades-old conflict between the ethnic Turks and Greeks constitutes a maddening stumbling block to Turkish security integration with Europe and NATO. Can Turkey and its neighbors find a way to get past this leftover conflict from the Cold War era, or will an island the size of Delaware continue to drive a wedge between Turkey and the West? The Cyprus issue has been festering for decades now, but Cypriot financial woes and recent gas finds in the Eastern Mediterranean could change the game, if the profits are presented as a sweetener for the island's unification. Still just as likely, these shocks could fuel worsening acrimony, especially as Turkey lays claim to hydrocarbon wealth that overlaps with Cypriot claims. On the other hand, a unification deal backed by the promise of revenue-sharing from natural gas wealth could bring the Cypriots together and thus elimate a hurdle ahead of Turkey's EU accession. This would also clear the way for cooperation between Israel, Turkey, and Cyprus on the pipeline to deliver gas to Europe.

Ties with Israel

On the heels of the Turkish-Israeli diplomatic rapprochement that was announced in March 2013, a natural gas deal could also help bring Turkey and Israel together. The Israelis have discovered large gas deposits off their shore, and Turkey is the most logical market from which to export this gas to international markets once production in the Israeli fields comes online. First, however, Turkey and Israel need to learn to trust one another again. The Israelis have watched Turkey's recent ascendancy with growing trepidation. Much to their chagrin, Turkey's new foreign policy has shed its former Kemalist-Western trappings. Nevertheless, Turkey's rise need not spell disaster for Israel. Ironically Turkey's new ambitions in the global arena have made integration into the community of Western powers more important than ever. Still, Turkey can become a regional and potentially global power only if it successfully reintegrates itself into the Western system. In this respect the crisis in Turkish-Israeli ties is a central test, gauging its ability to set a new course while remaining in the "sweet spot" between East and West.

The Arab Spring provides a strong incentive for reconciliation; Middle East unrest has challenged Turkey's "zero problems with neighbors" policy, casting Turkey and Syria as adversaries. At the same time, the region's revolutionary tremors have shaken the cornerstones of Israel's national security, even raising doubts about the future of its peace agreement with Egypt.

Moreover, both Israel and Turkey fear that a powerful Iran could fill the void in the region. The Turks are increasingly worried about what they regard as an Iran-sponsored Shiite axis spanning the region. Meanwhile, the Israelis feel that their window to stop Iran's nuclear program is closing.

The two countries share similar concerns about Syria and a desire to see the government of Bashar al-Assad out of power. After some equivocation Israel now prefers the devil it doesn't know; there is broad consensus among Israeli officials that the end of the Assad government would deal a blow to Iran and could dissolve the anti-Israeli axis binding Iran, Syria, and Hezbollah, the politically powerful Shiite militant group in Lebanon.

After a decade of warming to Syria's ruler, Turkey over the past year has begun to confront Syria. It not only hosts the opposition to the Assad regime, including the civilian Syrian National Council, but it is also arming some elements in the Free Syrian Army. Turkey has made it clear that Assad has to go, but it needs American support to play a more assertive role in the coalition against Assad. However, because Turkey fears that it might be left alone in conflict, it has shied away from deeper engagement, like setting up safe zones that might invite direct confrontation with Syria. That is, in part, a result of Washington's own cautious Syria policy, which has relied on United Nations diplomacy rather than direct measures to support the armed opposition.

Turkey seems interested in intervention inside Syria only if America and NATO back such an endeavor. Turkish-Israeli dialogue on Syria could bolster Israel's interest in regime change and enlist Israel to generate American support. A normalized relationship would also open opportunities for cooperation against the Assad government, with the Turks taking the political and regional lead and the Israelis providing intelligence and additional practical assets. The parties could also address shared concerns over the fate of the huge suspected chemical weapons stockpiles in Syria.

And there are ample economic foundations for rebuilding bilateral ties. Turkish-Israeli economic ties took off in the late-1990s as part of a growing strategic convergence. Deepening trade was underpinned by a series of bilateral agreements opening Turkish and Israeli markets to each other. Notable agreements included a free trade agreement (1996), a double-taxation prevention treaty (1997), and a bilateral investment treaty (1998). These agreements ushered in an era of improving political and economic ties. Trade jumped from $449 million in 1996 to more than $1.2 billion in 2002. This remarkable acceleration continued with bilateral trade increasing 14.6 percent per year, on average, from 2002 to 2008.

These ties were resilient in the face of diplomatic crisis, such as the boycott announced by several Israeli grocery chains in the wake of the 2010 Mavi Marmara flotilla incident. Despite the assertions on the part of these retailers, Turkish exports of vegetable products were unaffected by the announcement, and exports of prepared foodstuffs, beverages, and tobacco continued their ascent, doubling between 2007 and 2011. From 2010 to 2011 trade increased by 30.7 percent, far surpassing the growth that occurred during the heyday of Turkish-Israeli ties.

Managing the Syrian Conflict

The close relationship that President Obama has built with Prime Minister Erdogan has provided the United States with a key Muslim ally in the Middle East. As the crisis in Syria has deepened, the White House has appeared willing to wait for the demise of Syrian president Bashar al-Assad. For Ankara, the crisis has become an emergency. As turmoil in Syria has grown, Ankara has presumed that the United States and Turkey were on the same page regarding regime change. However, later on differences began to emerge, with the United States. deciding to lead from behind in Syria.

Ankara, however, wants an accelerated process. Particularly with the Syrian crisis threatening to spill into Turkey, Ankara feels the heat of the crisis next door—Erdogan has reason to believe that time is not on his side. As serious as these policy differences are, they are not likely to rupture Turkey's relationship with Washington, upon which Turkey greatly relies. Increasingly wary of Iran's regional ambitions, Erdogan knows that Tehran's Shiite regime militarily supports the Assad regime and the government of Iraqi Shiite Prime Minister Nouri al-Maliki, whom Ankara detests. The tumult of the Arab Spring has led Ankara to host the NATO missile-defense project as a bulwark against Iran, as well as Russia and China. Still, given Obama and Erdogan's divergent policies on Syria, weathering this storm will test Turkey's ability to work constructively with the West.

The Muslim Brotherhood

The Muslim Brotherhood has long been a force in Arab politics. Turkey's leaders have developed their religious affinities with this Sunni political network into political ties with some of these groups. In the wake of the Arab Spring these political movements have gained momentum, and now the Muslim Brotherhood and like-minded groups are growing as a force in Tunisia, Egypt, and Syria. As these groups vie for power, they will begin to show their hands on issues ranging from ties with Israel to minority rights—raising the potential of open disagreement with the West. In such a scenario Turkey may be torn between its Western values and the affinity its leaders have with their Sunni co-religionists. This could mean taking a milder tone toward policies the West simply cannot condone.

9 | Lessons for America

Turkey has many challenges, but it also has a lot going for it. In a recent interview with the *Wall Street Journal*, Demet Muftuoglu-Eseli, a liberal supporter of the arts and culture in Istanbul, expressed hope for the country's future, saying: "We made democracy work; we made a modern economy; we liberated women; we even have one of the world's top biennials. There is tension, but we'll overcome it."[1]

In many ways, this should bode well for the United States. A stable, confident Turkey could help shoulder some of the international burdens that until recently the United States has borne alone. But this will require a deeper understanding of just what Turkey can bring to the table. In Washington an energetic debate is already well underway on this topic.

THE "TURKISH MODEL": NOT SO EASY TO FOLLOW

Can the Turkish model of success, its challenges notwithstanding, be repeated in other Muslim majority countries?[2] How about countries experiencing the Arab Spring? And what role can Turkey play in encouraging and promoting democratic flourishing in these societies?

Arab societies are vastly different from Turkey. The first point, almost always overlooked in designating Turkey as a model, is that in Turkey the blend of Islamist politics and democracy took place within the context of sixty years of democratic experience.

This is not the case for Arab societies; most Arab countries are either still authoritarian or newly and shakily democratic. For instance, in all six Gulf Cooperation Council countries, plus Jordan and Morocco, monarchs remain more or less firmly in power—some with weak elected parliaments, some without even that. In Libya and Yemen autocrats have been deposed, but the new governments are not effectively in control and remain hostage to tribal, regional, or religious militias. In Iraq the elected government seems to be moving back to autocratic tendencies rather than turning away from them. Syria is currently locked in a bloody stalemate between a dictatorial regime and an increasingly violent popular uprising.

That leaves Tunisia and Egypt. In Tunisia, as in Turkey, a relatively moderate Islamist party won a majority in a free election but still has to compete with secular parties and social groups. Extreme fundamentalists are very rare. As my colleague David Pollock has explained, Tunisia's population is fairly well educated, with a large middle class.[3] The dominant Islamist party supports the private sector, including tourism and other international economic lifelines, and is cultivating the West. Tunisia may be the best prospect to follow in Turkey's footsteps. Tellingly Tunisia's ruling al-Nahda Party is the only Arab party that says it wants to emulate the Turkish model.

Egypt is a different story. The Muslim Brotherhood's party won a plurality in free elections, but its main competitors are the more extreme fundamentalist Salafi parties. The Brotherhood has tried to centralize political power, despite earlier promises of a more inclusive democratic approach. Egypt, sadly, also still suffers from widespread poverty and illiteracy—yet Egypt's new government has gone out of its way to alienate its friends in the United States and Europe over marginal issues like foreign NGOs. The Brotherhood has also publicly disavowed comparisons with the Turkish model.

Difficulties aside, Turkey has managed to attract much fanfare as a potential "model" for emerging Muslim societies in its neighborhood. Commentators on the Arab Spring have looked to Turkey as leading the curve of democratizing Muslim nations. But just how well does Turkey fit this mold? Vali Nasr, a leading scholar on Middle East politics, has championed the Turkish model argument. In his 2009 *Forces of Fortune*, Nasr delivers a sweeping tour of the rising bourgeoisie classes across the Muslim world. From the shopping malls of Dubai to the grassroots of Southeast Asia, Nasr shows how capitalism and Islam are coming together around the world to constitute a new force in global politics. According to Nasr, the implications of these commercial transformations are profound. Nasr claims that the growth of the middle class in Muslim societies is bound to produce more tolerant, liberal politics—a function of globalized Muslim populations adopting more worldly outlooks on society and politics. Just as it took Europe's Christian democrats many decades to reconcile fully with democracy, Muslim political forces will take time to come around, but Nasr holds that in the end they are bound to the road of democracy and liberalization. And Turkey is on the cutting edge in this development. According to Nasr, the Turkish model has "championed the most hopeful model in the region for both economic development and the liberalization of politics." This is because Turkey is the furthest along when it comes to melding Islam and capitalism, and this blend has resulted in a softer version of Islamic politics, as the AKP renounces the fundamentalist Islamic platforms of old.

Nasr gives a convincing account of how the Muslim middle class has the potential to lift societies out of the death grip of autocracy, without abandoning them to the tyranny of fundamentalism. But does this mean that Turkey's model of Muslim democracy is a recipe for liberal success? Perhaps, but not so fast.

As Nasr deftly illustrates, Muslim pragmatists have every reason to eschew the wild fantasies of the Islamists. After all, these extremist social structures are bad for business. But what happens next? For the Turkish case Nasr's answer is that "if Turkey stays on its current course, it will become a Muslim capitalist democracy." By this Nasr seems to imply some sort of practical coexistence between Islamic mores and democratic institutions, clearly more functional than a theocracy, but still a far cry from Denmark when it comes to Western liberal credentials. This outcome is certainly better than many other fates, but given Turkey's European and democratic accretions, why *can't* it aim for Denmark?

The AKP, for one, certainly seems to take this as the goal. The party's leaders are unambiguous that Turkey deserves nothing less than democracy writ large. AKP election pledges tout "advanced democracy" as the finish line for Turkey, a goal that denotes the highest standards in human rights, democratization, and civil society conditions. If the AKP acknowledges that nothing less is satisfactory for Turkey, then why should anything less be expected?

The real question is whether Turkey's ruling conservatives are willing to really commit to this path, pushing the envelope beyond the ad hoc cohabitation of democracy and Islam and pressing for a fully liberal society. In Turkey this question still remains unanswered. Of course, Turkish society is voicing these demands more loudly than ever, as witnessed during the 2013 Gezi movement. But it remains unclear if Turkey's leadership will be able to deliver on these demands. In fact, by many measures Turkey's course over the past decade has not been a straight shot toward liberal democracy.

It could even be argued that in certain respects Turkey is moving farther from liberal values, not closer. For one, even as Turkey's Muslim bourgeoisie has moved up the income ladder, the government's treatment of the press has not improved. In fact, based on analysis from Reporters Without Borders—a global press freedoms advocate—Turkey's press freedom took a sharp downward turn during the heyday of Turkey's economic boom, dropping from rank 99 worldwide in 2002 to 148 in 2011. In fact, it is difficult to say that Turkey's synthesis of Islam and economic liberalization has been accompanied by a marked improvement in political conditions overall. Freedom House has ranked Turkey as only "partly free" for the better part of the past decade, without any marked improvement, even as Turkey's middle class has gotten richer and Islam has more confidently entered the mainstream.

In terms of gender equality, Turkey's economic success has not had as positive an effect as might have been expected. Overall, Turkey is still far from a model to be emulated when it comes to women's empowerment. Not counting unpaid agricultural workers, only 22 percent of Turkey's women participate in the labor force.[4] This is only 4 percentage points higher than in 1988. In other words Turkey's economic

TABLE 6. Turkey: More Prosperous, Less Liberal

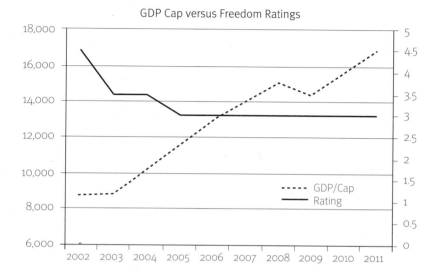

GDP Cap versus Freedom Ratings

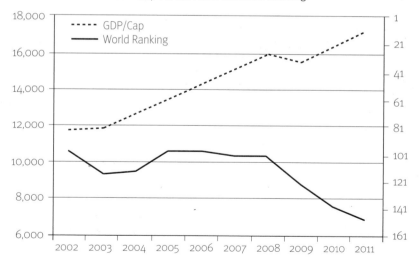

GDP Cap versus Press Freedom Ranking

Source: Strategic Report on Turkey. Washington Institute for Near East Policy.

boom has not revolutionized the role of women. In 2012 Turkey was ranked 65th in the world on the *Economist*'s Women's Opportunity Economic Index, a composite measure of women's access to education, workplace opportunity, finance, and legal rights. Turkey fell just behind countries like Namibia, Belarus, and Kazakhstan, while Bosnia, a European Muslim-majority country with an Ottoman heritage, beat Turkey by a wide margin. Of the 31 countries in Turkey's income range, Turkey is ranked 25th.[5] Needless to say, this trajectory should give us pause before concluding that Turkey has the ability to stand as a beacon for the emerging societies of the Arab world.

Turkey's status does not suggest, however, that the nation should not play a role in the Arab countries to promote democracy. Turkey can play a role in post-authoritarian Arab societies. Once again, this depends on how Ankara plays its hand and if Washington and Turkey's European allies do the right thing.

For starters, Turkey is better positioned than before to engage with Arab countries. Following the collapse of the Ottoman Empire, modern Turkey became a nation-state, turning toward Europe and abandoning the Middle East. During the last decade, along with Turkey's record-breaking economic growth, its foreign policy has shifted. It is no longer a poor country desperately seeking accession to the EU. Indeed, as political turmoil paralyzes the Middle East and economic meltdown devastates much of Mediterranean Europe, Turkey (together with France) is the only country in the region that has been spared.

Prior to the Arab Spring Turkey's foreign policy had shifted away from Europe, building Turkey more influence in the Middle East. After coming to power in 2002, the AKP cultivated ties with former Ottoman lands in the Middle East. The hope was that this would jump-start integration between Turkey and its neighbors, creating something like the 1950s "Benelux" bloc of Belgium, the Netherlands, and Luxembourg. For instance, of the thirty-one new Turkish diplomatic missions opened in the past decade, eleven are in Muslim and African countries.

This has resulted in new commercial and political ties, often at the expense of Turkey's ties with Europe. New trade patterns have led to the emergence of a more socially conservative business elite based in central Turkey, which derives strength from trading beyond Europe and is using its new wealth to push for a redefinition of Turkey's traditional approach to secularism. Since 2002 Ataturk's French-inspired model promoting freedom *from* religion in government, education, and politics has collapsed. Instead, the AKP and its allies have promoted a softer form of secularism that allows for freedom *of* religion. This has made the Turkish model appealing to socially conservative Arab countries, which, for the most part, regard French-style secularism as anathema.

In the past decade Turkey has also built soft power in Arab countries in the hope of rising up as a regional leader. This influence has accrued as Turkish businesses and grassroots organizations established networks and founded state-of-the-art high schools, run by the Sufi Islam-inspired Gulen Movement, to educate the future Arab elites.

Until the Arab Spring, this policy seemed to be inconclusive, largely because of the hard reality on the ground: Turkey's counterparts in rapprochement were not its neighboring peoples, but rather their undemocratic regimes. Now the Arab Spring is providing Turkey with an unprecedented opportunity to spread its influence further in newly free Arab societies.

Syria is a case in point: Whereas Ankara hoped to reach out to the Syrian people; the Assad regime took advantage of its close ties with Turkey, a member of NATO, to gain legitimacy while oppressing its people. The Arab Spring has ended the mirage. Even though Ankara repeatedly asked Assad to stop killing civilians, he chose to ignore these calls, demonstrating that Ankara had been unsuccessful in establishing soft power over Damascus.

Subsequently Ankara has dropped Assad, emerging instead as the chief regional opponent of his policies. This is Ankara's new policy toward the Arab Middle East: leading the world in dropping dictators in favor of the pro-democracy movements, from Egypt to Libya to Syria. Foreign Minister Davutoglu has trumpeted this cause loudly, proclaiming:

A new Middle East is being born. We will continue to be this Middle East's guardian, pioneer, and servant. In this new Middle

East, oppression and dictatorship will rule no more. It will be the public will, the public voice, and the voice of justice that is in command. Turkey will be a vocal defender of this voice.[6]

Accordingly, Turkey now has a chance to promote democracy in the Middle East and rise to leadership in the region.

BUILDING THE DEMOCRATIC CENTER: THE GERMAN MODEL

The role played by Germany in Portugal after that country exited the Salazar dictatorship in 1974 provides food for thought for future Turkish involvement in Arab countries. On April 25, 1974, the "Carnation Revolution" shook Portugal's forty-two-year-old dictatorship. A group of army officers, joined by the masses and an underground communist movement, rebelled against the regime. Surprisingly, the dictatorship collapsed like a house of cards. Portugal—then ridden by poverty, illiteracy, and authoritarianism—found itself at a crossroads: military rule or communist takeover? Neither happened. Thanks to the often-unmentioned efforts by Germany's Social Democratic Party (SPD) government and the Stiftungen (NGOs linked to Germany's political parties) to build centrist forces in Lisbon, the unexpected occurred: Portugal became a democracy.

In many ways Portugal in the 1970s parallels some of today's Arab societies. Arab countries, similarly poor and undemocratic, also stand at a crossroads, faced with the choice between military rule and an illiberal—in most cases radical Islamist—takeover.

In the 1970s, Germany's SPD, the first elected social-democratic government in Bonn, had the ability to uphold social democracy as a legitimate alternative to communism in Lisbon. Turkey can play a similar role in the Middle East today, if Ankara's first Islamist-rooted and democratically elected party, the AKP, encourages alternatives to radical Islamist parties.

In 1974 Portugal lacked deep democratic traditions and a sizable middle class. The powerful communist movement stood ready to hijack the revolution, while the military—which took charge after the dictatorship—seemed lost. The situation looked bleak. Only a few years later, however, Portugal blossomed as a democracy and later entered the EU. It is now one of the world's liberal democracies.

To facilitate this transformation the German government contributed to the fostering of a political center in Portugal: The SPD helped found the Portuguese Socialist Party (PS), a social-democratic movement that called for a democratic Portugal and the defeat of communist efforts to take power, in Bad Munstereifel, Germany. Furthermore Germany took the lead in organizing the "Friendship Solidarity Committee for Portuguese Democracy and Socialism" in August 1975. Led by German chancellor Willy Brandt, this committee included leading European social democrats, such as Swedish prime minister Olof Palme and Austrian Chancellor Bruno Kreisky, and became a platform in which social democrats shared knowledge with the PS and developed strategies for successful democratic transformation. The committee also prepared the groundwork for Portugal's EU membership.

The German Stiftungen also performed a valuable function. SPD-affiliated Friedrich Ebert Stiftung provided financial assistance to the PS, alone donating 10 to 15 million German marks for campaign training and the funding of PS leaders' travel, using discreet Swiss bank accounts to facilitate monetary transfers. Stiftungen connected to liberal and conservative German parties built counterparts in Portugal as well.

Ankara needs help to play Germany's role. Just as Bonn received financial and political assistance from the United States and other democracies in building Portuguese democracy, Turkey would benefit from support from the West as well as other Muslim-majority democracies, such as Indonesia, especially in creating "Turkish Stiftungen," the missing part of the Germany-Turkey parallel.

YET CHALLENGES REMAIN

Turkey ruled the Arab Middle East until World War I, and it must now be careful about how its messages are perceived there. Arabs might be drawn to fellow Muslims, but the Turks are also former imperial masters. Arabs are pressing for democracy, and if Turkey behaves like a new imperial power, this approach will backfire. Arab liberals and Islamists alike regularly suggest that Turkey is welcome in the Middle East but should not dominate it.

Then, there is the problem of transferring the Turkish model to Arab countries. In September 2011, when Erdogan landed at Cairo's new airport terminal (built by Turkish companies), he was warmly met by joyous millions, mobilized by the Muslim Brotherhood. However, he soon upset his pious hosts by preaching about the importance of a secular government that provides freedom of religion, using the Turkish word *laïcité*—derived from the French word for "secularism." In Arabic this term translates as "irreligious." Erdogan's message may have been partly lost in translation, yet the incident illustrates the limits of Turkey's influence in more socially conservative audience.

TURKEY'S TASKS

Ankara also faces domestic challenges that could hamper its influence in the Arab Spring. At the moment Turkey is debating chartering its first civilian-made constitution. If Turkey wants to become a true beacon of democracy in the Middle East, its new constitution must provide broader individual rights for the country's citizens and also eliminate limits on freedoms, such as strict censorship of the media.

Grant Constitutionally Mandated Collective Rights for Christians and Jews

Turkey has to grant constitutionally enshrined collective rights to Turkey's religious minorities. This move is necessitated by the way Turkey has historically regarded its non-Muslim groups. As inheritors of the Ottoman religious *millet* system, modern Turkey has in practice ascribed non-Muslims a separate status as minority groups. Even as Turkey modernized, this vestige remained, and Turkey's religious minorities were left facing discrimination from a state that was structured to subdue their communities. Even the most liberal of Turkey's institutions, the Ministry of Foreign Affairs, has long remained closed to religious minorities. Not a single Armenian or Jew holds a post in the ministry. In light of this history of discrimination against religious groups, the only way to truly emancipate Turkey's religious minorities is to recognize their status as disadvantaged entities and take measures accordingly, on a collective level. This means constitutionally recognized positive protections for these groups.[7]

In terms of specifics, there a few things the Turkish government could do right away to get the ball rolling. For example, Turkey's national identity cards continue to contain a box that specifies the citizen's religion. In the United States it seems absurd that authorities could require citizens to carry cards that say, "I'm a Methodist," or "I'm Jewish," and so forth, but Turkey currently requires just this. In order to truly become a religion-blind society, this practice has to end.

Create Equal Citizenship for Non-Muslims

More broadly, Turkey also needs constitutional clauses to ensure that public and government discrimination against the Christians and Jews ends. It also needs hate speech clauses to go after anti-Christian and anti-Jewish incitement. Ankara should also create an ombudsman who would oversee Jewish and Christian complaints of discrimination. Turkey also needs to update and improve its primary and secondary school curriculum. Even as much of Turkey's school curriculum is updated, vestiges of old prejudices remain that paint Turkish Christians and Jews as "un-Turkish" groups. Turkey must ensure that root-and-branch reform of its national curriculum is undertaken to instill in Turkey's next generations a positive view of Turkey's historical diversity. Finally, Ankara needs to launch a public campaign to raise awareness against anti-Semitism and anti-Christian feelings. If Turkey is to rise as a democracy, it has to treat all its citizens fairly and equally, including the twenty thousand Jews and seventy thousand Christians who are its citizens.

Build a New *Diyanet*

When dealing with politicized religion, Ataturk's major preoccupation was to keep radical influences out of religion and religion out of politics. Using the Ottoman tradition of subservience of Sunni Islam (personified in the office of the *Sheikh al-Islam*) to the sultan's rule, he established the official Directorate General for Religious Affairs (*Diyanet*) subject to government supervision. In this regard Ataturk and the *Diyanet* have been helped by the Turks' particular interpretation of Islam, historically rooted in the Sufi traditions of Central Asia, the Turks' homeland. Following the Turks' arrival in Anatolia (Turkey) in 1071, centuries of Turkish coexistence with Christians and Jews in Anatolia and then in the Balkans and Central Europe under the Ottoman Empire produced a specific version of Central Asian/Turkish/Balkan Islam. This brand of Islam, rooted in the liberal Hanefi-Maturidi tradition of religious jurisprudence, has created an environment in which the Turks have practiced Islam as a matter of personal faith, at peace with other surrounding faiths. In the modern age this evolution has produced a large group of Turks at ease with modernity and its various accouterments, including secularism. Helped by this legacy, the *Diyanet* has promoted a tolerant version of Islam. It also trained imams and managed mosques, keeping religion Turkish, under control, and for the most part (at least until the 1970s) outside the political sphere. The Ottoman tradition of subjugating the Islamic clergy to the sultan's power subsequently molded Turkish secularism. Ataturk's *laïcité* did not simply exclude religion from education and politics; it involved state influence over religion.

Even in the post-Kemalist age, the *Diyanet* serves a purpose in Turkey. As a government department the *Diyanet* builds mosques and pays imams' salaries. In turn, it fosters a moderate understanding of Islam. For all its advantages, though, this Ottoman-inspired model is not built to last in the twenty-first century. Designed to cater to Turkey's majority Sunni population, the institution does not offer the same support to Turkey's other faiths. If the *Diyanet* is to continue to play a role in Turkey's religious life, while also living up to the standards of contemporary liberal democracy, it will need to change its exclusive focus on the Sunni brand of Islam and open its doors, staff, as well as its budget, to other branches of Islam, such as the Shiites (Turkey has over a million Shiites of Azeri origin who live in the country's northeast and in Istanbul), to non-orthodox Muslims, such as Alevis, as well as Christians

and Jews, and to other faiths that Turks decide they wish to profess.[8]
The new *Diyanet* ought to be stripped of its exclusive Muslim clergy
character. This new *Diyanet,* with Muslims, Jews, Christians, and others at its helm, should equally fund and support the religious and spir-
itual activities of all these groups. This is the best way to ensure that
non-Sunni Muslims as well as non-Muslims feel that they are equally
treated by the Turkish state.

Guarantee More Individual Rights for Everyone, Including the Kurds

Turkey needs to provide its citizens with the broadest individual freedoms imaginable if it is to satisfy its Kurdish citizens about their rights.
With this strategy, the AKP can win rights for the Kurds, while also sat-
isfying the broader populace. Many Turks are uncomfortable with the
country's current military-written constitution that reads like a boarding school's "don't do" list. Not just the Kurds, but Turks of all stripes
would welcome a fresh constitution that lists their freedoms and just
that. This is the best way to make Turkey a liberal democracy. It is also
the best fit for the Kurdish *Weltschmerz.*

A prescription for individual rights is also most appropriate because
of Turkey's historical experience. In contrast to religious minorities,
Turkey's Muslim ethnic minorities were never categorized separately
in Turkey's political sphere or discriminated against because of their
identities. In this respect Turkey's Kurds are not a minority *sensu stricto.*
Moreover, Kurds have not faced the same sort of societal discrimination. They have, for example, never been barred from office or assigned
a subcitizen status. Kurds have held posts at every level of government.
The forms of repression they have endured took different forms as the
result of distinct historical circumstances. For this reason the griev-
ances of Turkey's Kurdish population can most aptly be addressed by
strengthening the framework of individual rights, an approach that
would be embraced by Kurds and Turks alike.

There are a number of specific steps the government could take right
away to get off to a strong start. First, a very feasible goal would be to
remove the legal uncertainties that surround using indigenous names

for villages and landmarks, a change that would be welcome not only by the Kurds but by many other linguistically non-Turkish communities as well. During the twentieth century, many of the names of buildings, towns, and streets were renamed with "Turkish" names to replace the names that came from Armenian, Georgian, Syriac, Kurdish, or Greek sources. During the 1960s, for instance, one-third of the place-names in Turkey were replaced in this manner, and following the 1980 military coup the state redoubled its efforts to eradicate these names from the historical record.[9] For the Kurds in Turkey's far southeast, having to use these Turkish names serves as a constant reminder of cultural repression. The AKP has shown a positive attitude toward this problem, and AKP leaders have even used indigenous names when addressing crowds in the southeast, showcasing their liberal attitude. But laws remain on the books that technically make it possible to prosecute local government leaders for using Kurdish names in public. This lack of consistency has undercut some of the goodwill the AKP has garnered with its language policies. The government would do well by changing these laws and providing clear legal protections for indigenous place-names to exist alongside the names currently in use.

Changing judicial culture should be a goal as well, even if it takes time. Turkish criminal law can often be vague in wording, gaining much of its significance from how technical and legal terms are interpreted by the judges reviewing a case. Even if criminal statutes may seem perfectly reasonable if interpreted prudently, some Turkish judges have gained a reputation for illiberal interpretations of the law. This factor has been behind many of the harsh rulings against political activists and journalists in Turkey. Turkey can fix this by putting more emphasis on training its judges in European practices and standards, inculcating its judges with a more liberal framework with which to interpret the existing laws. This simple step could go a long way in improving the quality of Turkey's judiciary.

Finally, Turkey should revise its electoral laws to give Kurdish parties a secure voice. Current Turkish electoral laws bar any party that does not attain at least 10 percent of the popular vote from entering parliament. Other countries in Europe have minimum thresholds as well, but Turkey's 10 percent is beyond the pale, especially because its primary function has become to block the Kurdish nationalist BDP from running as a party in elections. Instead, they have to work around the rule by entering parliament as independents. Turkey should lower its 10 percent threshold to a more reasonable 5 percent, which seems to be the most common practice in European democracies. This compromise would still prevent too many tiny parties from taking seats in the chamber, fragmenting the lawmaking process. However, it would also allow the democratic process to function better and give Kurdish voices a more established seat at the table.

WILL TURKEY RISE FURTHER?

Turkey's relative stability at a time when the region is in upheaval is attracting investment from less stable neighbors like Iran, Iraq, Syria, and Lebanon. Ultimately political stability and regional clout are Turkey's hard cash, and its economic growth will depend on both. Turkey will rise as a regional power as well as play a role in the region only if it sets a genuine example as a liberal democracy and continues to build its hallmark of soft power. Turkey will also need to bring to completion Davutoglu's vision of a "zero problems" foreign policy. This means moving forward to rebuild strong ties with Israel and getting along with the Greek Cypriots, as well as normalizing ties with Armenia and keeping Iran at bay. Turkey has a long way to go if it is to achieve this goal, but there are a number of tasks that Turkey can get started on right away.

Turkey is rising. It is the wealthiest large Muslim-majority state. It is part of Europe but is also interlinked with Muslim countries. It has strong ties to global institutions, including NATO, IMF, OECD, and the Council of Europe, and it is the only Muslim-majority country that has a seat in all these bodies. With stars aligned in its favor, only Turkey can prevent its rise to become a global player. If Turkey moves in the right direction, it will keep its Western overlay strong, write a liberal constitution, and build sway among Muslim countries, benefiting from the ensuing economic growth and political stability. If it does not play its hand correctly, however, Turkey could face tremendous instability, including economic meltdown, a rise in political violence, shaky governments, and even conflict with neighbors. If this happens, the Turks could again become the sick man of Europe. The ball is in the Turks' court.

Notes

INTRODUCTION

1. Turkey's average individual consumption (AIC) stands at 60, when the European average is set at 100. Eurostat, 2012, "GDP per capita in the Member States ranged from 45 percent to 274 percent of the EU27 average in 2011," accessible at "GDP per Capita, Consumption per Capita and Price Level Indices," http://epp.eurostat .ec.europa.eu/statistics_explained/index.php/GDP_per_capita,_consumption_per _capita_and_price_level_indices.

2. "GDP per Capita."

3. World Bank, 2012, "World Bank Databank", http://databank.worldbank.org/ddp/ home.do?Step=1&id=4.

4. Some experts suggest that Turkey may have hit the middle income trap. "Experts See Long-Term Turkish Economic Growth," *Today's Zaman*, September 24, 2012, http://www.todayszaman.com/news-293322-experts-see—long-term-turkish -economic-growth.html.

5. Jean-Pierre Lehmann, "Turkey's 2023 Economic Goal in Global Perspective," EDAM, http://edam.org.tr/eng/document/Lehmann-June%202011.pdf.

6. *Middle income trap* can be defined as a plateau in which rising labor costs and the inability to bring in high-tech industries results in lethargic growth for emerging economies after such economies initially witness high growth rates thanks to low labor costs and their ability to attract investment in labor-intensive industries. Çağlar, "European Union."

7. "FDI in Turkey," Invest in Turkey: The Republic of Turkey Prime Ministry Investment Support and Promotion Agency, 2011, http://www.invest.gov.tr/en-US/ investmentguide/investorsguide/pages/FDIinTurkey.aspx.

8. Gürsel, "Controversial Outlook of Turkish Economy."

9. Gürsel, "Controversial Outlook of Turkish Economy."

10. Turkish Foreign Ministry, 2012, "Afrika Ülkeleri İle İlişkiler," Türkiye Cumhuriyeti Dışişleri Bakanlığı, http://www.mfa.gov.tr/turkiye-afrika-iliskileri.tr.mfa.

11. World Bank, 2012, "World Bank Databank," http://databank.worldbank.org/ddp/home.do?Step=1&id=4.

12. Peker, "Turkey Gets Ratings Boost."

13. Turkish Statistical Institute, "Gross Domestic Product according to the Periods and the Branches of the Activity (With the Constant Prices 1998 Base Year)," 2012, http://www.turkstat.gov.tr/VeriBilgi.do?alt_id=55.

14. This may have changed following the Ergenekon case, which started in 2007. Facing allegations of a coup plot against the AKP government, around a quarter of Turkey's generals have landed in jail, and the effectiveness of today's Turkish military is yet to be tested on the battlefield.

15. Measure in PPP, The World Bank, "World DataBank," http://databank.worldbank .org/data/views/reports/tableview.aspx?isshared=true.

16. "Derviş'ten 2023 hedefi için üç uyarı," NTVMSNBC, September 27, 2012, http:// www.ntvmsnbc.com/id/25385425/.

1. TURKEY'S NEW WORLD

1. Daniel Dombey, "Turkey's 8.8% Growth Beats Expectations," *Financial Times*, September 10, 2011, http://www.ft.com/intl/cms/s/0/f4504c54-dd32-11e0-b4f2 -00144feabdc0.html#axzz2YSvoK0

2. "Robust Private Sector Gives Turkey Fastest H1 Growth Worldwide," *Today's Zaman*, September 12, 2012, http://www.todayszaman.com/news-256556-robust -private-sector-gives-turkey-fastest-h1-growth-worldwide.html.

3. "Milyonerler kulübüne 1 yılda 9 bin 755 milyoner eklendi," *Cumhuriyet*, December 10, 2011, http://www.cumhuriyet.com.tr/?hn=299468; World Bank, 2012, "World Bank Databank," http://databank.worldbank.org/ddp/home.do?Step=1&id=4.

4. Turkstat, "Foreign Trade Statistics," http://www.turkstat.gov.tr/PreTablo.do?alt _id=10465.

5. Çetindamar and Kozanoğlu, *Competitiveness of Turkish Hidden Champions*, 2074.

6. Çetindamar and Kozanoğlu, *Competitiveness of Turkish Hidden Champions*, 2074.

7. "Kurum Bilgisi," Casper, http://www.casper.com.tr/hakkimizda.

8. "Turkish Automotive Industry Report," Turkish Investment Support and Promotion Agency, August 2010, http://www.invest.gov.tr/en-US/infocenter/publications/ Documents/AUTOMOTIVE.INDUSTRY.pdf.

9. "Foreign Trade," Invest in Turkey, http://www.invest.gov.tr/en-US/investment guide/investorsguide/Pages/InternationalTrade.aspx.

10. "Turkey-Mauritius Free Trade Agreement," Turkish Foreign Ministry, http://www .economy.gov.tr/index.cfm?sayfa=tradeagreements&bolum=fta&country=MU &region=0.

11. Turkstat, "Foreign Trade Statistics," http://www.turkstat.gov.tr/PreTablo.do?alt_id=1046.

12. Turkstat, "Foreign Trade Statistics."

13. "Türkiye Siyasi Gündem Araştırması," Andy-AR, January 2012.

14. "Country statistical profile: Turkey 2013," OECD, June 2013, http://www.oecd-ilibrary.org/; "Turkey to Decrease Debt Burden to 37 pct in 2012," *Hurriyet Daily News*, September 27, 2012, http://www.hurriyetdailynews.com/turkey- to-decrease-debt-burden- to-37-pct-in-2012.aspx?pageID=238&nID=24944&NewsCatID=344.

15. "FDI in Turkey," Invest in Turkey, http://www.invest.gov.tr/en-us/investmentguide/investorsguide/pages/FDIinTurkey.aspx.

16. Türk Hava Yolları Yıllık Raporu, 2011, http://www.turkishairlines.com/download/investor_relations/annual_reports/2011_Faaliyet_Raporu.pdf.

17. "Turkey," CIA World Fact Book, 2013, https://www.cia.gov/library/publications/the-world-factbook/geos/tu.html.

18. United Nations Department of Economic and Social Affairs, "World Urbanization Prospects, the 2011 Revision" (2012).

19. "Suriye'den 1.8 milyar TL geldi!," Haberturk, October 1, 2012, http://ekonomi.haberturk.com/makro-ekonomi/haber/781235-suriyeden- 18-milyar-tl-geldi.

2. CONSERVATIVE ISLAM MEETS CAPITALISM

1. Kayseri Municipality, http://www.kayseri.gov.tr/default_Bo.aspx?content=217.

2. "Why Kayseri," Kayseri Chamber of Industry, 2012, http://www.kayso.org.tr/folders/18480/categorial1docs/12234/Neden%20Kayseri%20EN.pdf.

3. Greek prime minister Konstantinos Karamanlis's family originates from Karaman outside Kayseri, suggesting that the leader of Greece had at one time Turkish-speaking parents, hence Mr. Karamanlis's last name.

4. For decades the authorities had turned a blind eye to requests to make improvements to the culture landmark.

5. Hakan Yavuz, "Ethical Not Shari'a Islam: Islamic Debates in Turkey," *Review of Faith in International Affairs* 10, no. 4.

6. Yavuz, "Ethical Not Shari'a Islam."

7. Binnaz Toprak, Irfan Bozan, Tan Morgül, and Nedim Şener, *Being Different in Turkey: Religion, Conservatism, and Otherization* (New York: Open Society Foundations, 2009).

8. Alevis are a community in Turkey who profess a liberal understanding of Islam; for more on the Alevis, see chapter 6.

9. Toprak, "Political Power."

10. "Everything for Turkey: AK Party Election Manifesto," 2002.

11. "Mortality rate, infant," World Bank, http://data.worldbank.org/indicator/SP.DYN.IMRT.IN.

12. "Mortality rate, infant."
13. "Health expenditure per capita," World Bank, http://data.worldbank.org/indicator/ SH.XPD.PCAP.
14. "Academic Ranking of Universities in the OIC," SESRIC.org, April 2007, http://www .sesric.org/imgs/news/Image/RankUniv.ppt.
15. "Patent Applications, Residents," World Bank, http://data.worldbank.org/indicator/ IP.PAT.RESD/countries/GB-TR?display=graph.
16. "Innovation Statistics," Turkstat, http://www.turkstat.gov.tr/PreTablo.do?alt _id=1039.
17. "Dindar bir gençlik yetiştirmek istiyoruz!" Habertürk, February 1, 2012, http:// www.haberturk.com/gundem/haber/711672-dindar-bir-genclik-yetistirmek -istiyoruz-.

3. THE MILITARY GETS ON BOARD

1. For more on the Alevis, see chapter 6.
2. Zarakol, *After Defeat*.
3. Zarakol, *After Defeat*.
4. Hale, *Turkish Politics and the Military*.
5. While Ottoman military westernization moved full steam ahead, outside the military sphere the quest for westernization progressed in a piecemeal manner. Still, the empire created many nonmilitary Western and secular institutions, such as the School of Administrative Sciences (Mekteb-i Mulkiye), founded in 1859 to train administrative officers and diplomats—this school would later give Turkey a fully Western, secular diplomatic corps, the basis of today's Ministry of Foreign Affairs. Over time the Ottoman bureaucracy became mostly secularized and westernized and joined in the efforts to promote westernization.
6. Jenkins, "Continuity and Change."
7. "Turks Downbeat about Their Institutions: Even Military Less Well-Regarded," Pew Research Center, September 7, 2010, http://pewresearch.org/pubs/1720/ poll-turkey-referendum-constitution-confidence-institutions-erdogan-negative -rating-nations.
8. "Military's April 27 Memorandum Relegated to Dustbin of History," *Today's Zaman*, August 29, 2011, http://www.todayszaman.com/newsDetail_getNewsById.action ;jsessionid=6CF7C9BCDE23BCFCED90562C1A657CCC?newsId=255269.
9. "Cemil Çiçek'in açıklamasının tam metni," NTVMSNBC, April 18, 2007.
10. Letsch, "Turkey Military Chiefs."
11. "Turks Downbeat about Their Institutions"; Düzel, "Adil Gür."
12. "Kılıçdaroğlu'ndan Cevap: 'Yüzde 99 Değil 99.5 Sabotaj,'" TRT *Haber*, September 11, 2012, http://www.trthaber.com/haber/gundem/kilicdaroglundan-cevap-yuzde -99-degil-995-sabotaj-55284.html.

13. "Böyle bir ordu PKK'yı yenebilir mi?" *Zaman,* June 20, 2010, http://www.zaman
    .com.tr/newsDetail_getNewsById.action?haberno=1006756&keyfield=.

14. "AKP'den Özel'e tam destek," Ulusal Kanal, October 11, 2012, http://www.ulusal
    kanal.com.tr/gundem/akpden-ozele-tam-destek-h6017.html

4. IS TURKISH POWER MYTH OR REALITY?

1. Vicky, "Turkey Moves into Africa."

2. "Somalia Famine: Turkish PM Erdogan Visits Mogadishu," BBC News, August 19,
   2011, http://www.bbc.co.uk/news/world-africa-14588960.

3. "'Hedef olağan durumda 80, iyimser durumda 110 milyon turist olmalıdır,'" *Tur-
   izmGuncel,* June 28, 2012, http://www.turizmguncel.com/haber/hedef-olagan
   -durumda-80-iyimser-durumda-110-milyon-turist-olmalidir-h11352.html; "Tourism Highlights," World Tourism Organization, 2012, http://mkt.unwto.org/sites/
   all/files/docpdf/unwtohighlights12enlr_1.pdf.

4. "'Hedef olağan durumda 80.'"

5. Turkstat, "Turizm Istatistikleri," http://tuikapp.tuik.gov.tr/turizmapp/menuturizm
   .zul.

6. Öcek, "Number of Libyan Tourists."

7. Tamimi, "Turkey Emerges as Tourism Hotspot."

8. World Bank, 2012, "World Bank Databank", http://databank.worldbank.org/ddp/
   home.do?Step=1&id=4.

9. Akgün and Gündoğar, *Perception of Turkey.*

10. Telhami, "Annual Arab Public Opinion Survey: 2011."

11. İdiz, "PM Erdoğan's Surprising Message."

12. "Turkey Raises Pressure on Syria," *Al Jazeera,* August 10, 2011, http://www
    .aljazeera.com/news/middleeast/2011/08/2011891785050404477.html.

13. Weiss, "Syrian Rebels Say Turkey."

14. "2 bin PKK'lı Suriye'nin Kurmên Dağları'na yerleşti", *Milliyet,* March 29, 2012,
    http://gundem.milliyet.com.tr/2-bin-pkk-li-suriye-nin-kurm-n-daglari-na-yerlesti/
    gundem/gundemdetay/29.03.2012/1521456/default.htm.

15. Enders, "Iran-Kurdish Rebel Ceasefire Holds."

16. "Gov't Unrelenting on Mop-up Operations against Terror despite Casualties,"
    Today's Zaman, September 16, 2012, http://www.todayszaman.com/mobile
    _detailn.action?newsId=292564.

17. "Tehran Denies Turkish Deputy PM's Accusations over PKK Support," *Today's
    Zaman,* August 13, 2012, http://www.todayszaman.com/newsDetail_getNews
    ById.action?newsId=289373.

18. For details on Ankara's less than hospitable treatment, see "Jalili Gets Cold Shoul-
    der," *Hurriyet Daily News,* September 19, 2012, http://www.hurriyetdailynews
    .com/jalili-gets-cold-shoulder.aspx?pageID=238&nID=30456&NewsCatID=338.

19. "Obama'dan Erdoğan'a: Anne acısını iyi bilirim," *Zaman*, November 5, 2012, http://www.zaman.com.tr/dunya_obamadan-erdogana-anne-acisini-iyi-bilirim _1198811.html.

5. BEYOND OTTOMAN BENEVOLENCE

1. Lately reforms that Turkey has carried out toward EU accession have led to an improvement in the non-Muslims' status. Since December 1999, when the EU recognized Turkey as a candidate country for membership, Ankara has moved fast to satisfy the EU's accession rules, Copenhagen Criteria, which stipulate among other things, "respect for minorities." This process has started a discussion on granting wider rights to the non-Muslims (as well as facilitating broadcasting and education in Kurdish and other languages spoken by various Muslim communities). For more on Turkey's EU reforms, see Soner Cagaptay, "European Union Reforms Diminish the Role."

2. For more on this controversy, see *Radikal*, October 13, 17, and 31, 1999, and *Hürriyet*, March 24, 2002.

3. Suna Çağaptay, "Frontierscape."

6. THE OTHER TURKEY

1. Esmer, *Türkiye Değerler Atlası*.

2. Esmer, *Türkiye Değerler Atlası*.

3. Rainsford, "Two Faces of Modern Turkey."

4. Karpat, *Millets and Nationality*. For case studies of nationalization through religion among the Balkan Christians see Poulton, *Who Are the Macedonians?*, 26–47; and Kitromilides, "'Imagined Communities,'" 149–92.

5. McCarthy, *Death and Exile*. On the other hand, Cem Behar notes that between 1876 and 1895, some 1,150,015 immigrants arrived in the Ottoman Empire. Behar, *Population of the Ottoman Empire and Turkey*, 51.

6. Karpat, "Historical Continuity and Identity Change," 22.

7. Ahmad, *Young Turks*.

8. McCarthy, *Arab World, Turkey and the Balkans*.

9. *İstatistik Yıllığı Üçüncü Cilt*, TÜİK, 2011, 57.

10. Yıldız, Ne Mutlu Türküm Diyebilene, 84.

11. Mardin, "Ottoman Empire," 115.

12. Mardin, "Ottoman Empire," 115.

13. "2011 Seçim Sonuçları," Seçim.Haberler.com, http://secim.haberler.com/2011/.

14. Bulut, "Arap Aleviliği (Nusayrilik) Anadolu Aleviliğinin nesidir?"

15. "The Position of Alevite Communities in Modern Turkey," Cem Vakfı, June 2005; "Alevis Call on the Turkish Government to Recognize and Respect Their Faith," *Sabah* (Istanbul), November 9, 2003.

16. U.S., Bureau of Democracy, Human Rights, and Labor, *Turkey*.

17. Çarkoğlu and Kalaycıoğlu, *Türkiye'de Siyasetin Yeni Yüzü*.

18. Kamil Fırat, "Kentleşen Alevilik" (Urbanizing Alevism), *Milliyet*, July 5, 2005, www.milliyet.com.tr/2005/07/05/guncel/guno1.html.

19. Soner Cagaptay, "No Women, No Europe"; Healy, Ozbilgin, and Aliefendioglu, "Academic Employment and Gender."

20 Soner Cagaptay, "No Women, No Europe."

21. Bendern, "One Million Turks."

22. For a comprehensive study of the emergent electoral patterns in Turkey, see Soner Cagaptay, Arifagaoglu, Outzen, and Menekse, "Turkey's New Political Landscape."

7. CAN TURKEY MAKE IT?

1. "55 milyon kişi 'etnik olarak' Türk," http://www.milliyet.com.tr/2007/03/22/guncel/agun.html.

2. Soner Cagaptay, *Islam, Secularism and Nationalism in Modern Turkey*.

3. Mardin, "Ottoman Empire," 115.

4. Soner Cagaptay, *Islam, Secularism and Nationalism in Modern Turkey*.

5. Because the Ottomans did not bother to reorganize the Kurdish lands after capturing them, *Kurdistan* was a geographic term and not a political one.

6. Dundar, *İttihat ve Terakki'nin Müslümanları İskân Politikası*.

7. Reynolds, *Shattering Empires*.

8. Turkish Statistical Institute, "Income and Living Conditions Survey, 2011."

9. Zeydanlıoğlu, "Turkey's Kurdish Language Policy."

10. "PM to Win Kurdish Hearts and Minds," *Hurriyet Daily News*, December 31, 2008.

11. "First Undergrad Kurdish Department Opens in SE," *Hurriyet Daily News*, September 24, 2012; "Kürtçe seçmeli ders olacakt," *Habertürk*, June 12, 2012, http://www.haberturk.com/gundem/haber/750142-kurtce-secmeli-ders-olacak.

12. According to a recent International Crisis Group report, between June 2011 and August 2012, PKK-related violence killed over seven hundred people.

13. "Turkey Falls into Parts on 'National Pride Map,'" *Hurriyet Daily News*, December 4, 2012.

14. "2011 Seçim Sonuçları," Seçim.Haberler.com, http://secim.haberler.com/2011/.

15. 2011 Seçim Sonuçları."

16. Barış ve Demokrasi Partisi: Parti Programimiz, http://bdpblog.wordpress.com/parti-programimiz/.

17. While previous presidents have been elected by the parliament, a 2007 amendment stipulated that the next president be elected in the ballot box.

18. Soner Cagaptay and Evans, "Turkey's Changing Relations with Iraq."

19. Gibbons, "Turkey's Enlightenment Languishes."

20. "The Ephemeral Alevi Opening," *Economist*, August 11, 2012, http://www
    .economist.com/node/21560314; "Turkey Drops Anti-abortion Legislation," *Al
    Jazeera*, June 22, 2012, http://www.aljazeera.com/news/europe/2012/06/
    2012622811474159.html.
21. "Turkey Tries Pianist Fazil Say for Insulting Islam," BBC, October 18, 2012, http://
    www.bbc.co.uk/news/world-europe-19990943.
22. Çarkoğlu and Rubin, *Religion and Politics in Turkey*.
23. "Türk Milyarderlerin Sayısı Azaldı," TRT, http://www.trthaber.com/haber/
    gundem/turk-milyarderlerin-sayisi-azaldi-31597.html.
24. For this section, I am indebted to collaboration with Parag Khanna.

8. IS THERE ROOM FOR TURKEY IN THE WEST?

1. Kinzer, "Ecevit, Ex-Skeptic, Leads Turkey's Switch."
2. "Turkey 2012 Progress Report," European Commission, October 10, 2012, http://
   ec.europa.eu/enlargement/pdf/key_documents/2012/package/tr_rapport_2012
   _en.pdf.
3. "Turkey's EU Bid Overshadows Angela Merkel Visit," BBC, March 29, 2010. "German, French Leaders Emphasize Opposition to Turkey Joining EU," *Hurriyet Daily
   News*, May 11, 2009.
4. This section is indebted to writing and collaboration with my colleague, Michael
   Herzog.

9. LESSONS FOR AMERICA

1. Osborne, "Dreaming in Ottoman."
2. For this section, I am indebted to David Pollock for his insight and collaboration.
3. Pollock and Soner Cagaptay, "What Happened to 'The Turkish Model'?"
4. İlkkaracan, "Why so Few Women in the Labor Market in Turkey?"
5. "Women's Economic Opportunity Index 2012."
6. Ahmet Davutoğlu, speech to the Turkish Parliamentary Assembly, April 2012.
7. For an illuminating study on minority policy in Turkey, see Netherlands Scientific
   Council for Government Policy, *European Union, Turkey and Islam*.
8. For an in-depth study on proposals to reform the *Diyanet* see Çakırand Bozan, *Sivil,
   Şeffaf ve Demokratik Bir Diyanet*.
9. Nişanyan, "Hayali Coğrafyalar."

Bibliography

Ahmad, Feroz. *The Young Turks: The CUP in Turkish Politics, 1908–1914.* Oxford: Oxford University Press, 1969.

Akgün, Mensur, and Sabiha Şenyücel Gündoğar. *The Perception of Turkey in the Middle East.* Istanbul: Turkish Economic and Social Studies Foundation (TESEV), 2011.

Barkey, Karen, and Mark Von Hagen. *After Empire: Multiethnic Societies and Nation-building: The Soviet Union and the Russian, Ottoman, and Habsburg Empires.* Boulder CO: Westview Press, 1997.

Behar, Cem, comp. *The Population of the Ottoman Empire and Turkey.* Historical Statistics Series, vol. 2. Ankara: State Institute of Statistics, 1996.

Bendern, Paul de. "One Million Turks Rally against Government." Reuters, April 29, 2009. http://www.reuters.com/article/2007/04/29/us-turkey-president-idUSL 2910950920070429.

Bulut, Halil İbrahim. "Arap Aleviliği (Nusayrilik) Anadolu Aleviliğinin nesidir?" *Zaman*, September 6, 2012. http://www.zaman.com.tr/newsDetail_getNewsById. action?haberno=1341543&title=yorum-halil-ibrahim-bulutarap-aleviligi-nusayrilik -anadolu-aleviliginin-nesidir&haberSayfa=1.

Cagaptay, Soner. "European Union Reforms Diminish the Role of the Turkish Military: Ankara Knocking on Brussels' Door." *Policywatch* no. 781 (August 12, 2003). Washington DC: Washington Institute for Near East Policy.

Cagaptay, Soner. *Islam, Secularism and Nationalism in Modern Turkey: Who Is a Turk.* New York: Routledge, 2006.

———. "No Women, No Europe." *Hurriyet Daily News*, January 20, 2010. http://www .washingtoninstitute.org/policy-analysis/view/no-women-no-europe.

Cagaptay, Soner, Hale Arifağaoğlu, Eva Outzen, and Bilge Menekse. "Turkey's New Political Landscape: Implications of the 2011 Elections." Washington DC: Washington Institute for Near East Policy, 2011.

Cagaptay, Soner, and Tyler Evans. *"Turkey's Changing Relations with Iraq: Kurdistan Up, Baghdad Down."* Washington DC: Washington Institute for Near East Policy. 2012.

Çağaptay, Suna. "Frontierscape: Reconsidering Bithynian Structures and Their Builders on the Byzantine-Ottoman Cusp." *Muqarnas*, 2011.

Çağlar, Esen. "The European Union Has to Be Turkey's Growth Story." Istanbul: Turkiye Ekonomi Politikalari Arastirma Vakfi (TEPAV), March 19, 2012. http://www.tepav.org.tr/en/kose-yazisi-tepav/s/3158.

Çakır, Ruşen, and İrfan Bozan. *Sivil, Şeffaf ve Demokratik Bir Diyanet İşleri Başkanlığı Mümkün mü??* Istanbul: TESEV, 2005.

Çarkoğlu, Ali, and Ersin Kalaycıoğlu. *Türkiye'de Siyasetin Yeni Yüzü*. Istanbul: Açık Toplum Enstitüsü, 2006.

Çarkoğlu, Ali, and Barry Rubin. *Religion and Politics in Turkey*. London: Routedge, 2004.

Çetindamar, D., and H. Kozanoğlu. *Competitiveness of Turkish Hidden Champions*. Istanbul: Sabanci University-PICMET, 2012.

Dundar, Fuat. *İttihat ve Terakki'nin Müslümanları İskân Politikası*. Istanbul: İletişim, 2002.

Düzel, Neşe. "Adil Gür: 'Orduya güven en düşük noktada,'" *Taraf*, January 23, 2010. http://www.taraf.com.tr/nesed-uzel/makale-adil-gur-orduya-guven-en-dusuk-noktada.htm.

Enders, David. "Iran-Kurdish Rebel Ceasefire Holds amid Skepticism." Pulitzer Center on Crisis Reporting, November 7, 2011. http://pulitzercenter.org/reporting/iraq-cease-fire-kurdish-rebels-iran-government.

Esmer, Yılmaz. *Türkiye Değerler Atlası*. Istanbul: Bahçeşehir Üniversitesi, 2012.

The European Union, Turkey and Islam. Amsterdam: Netherlands Scientific Council for Government Policy, 2004.

Gibbons, Fiachra. "Turkey's Enlightenment Languishes, like the Journalists in Its Prisons." *Guardian*, March 13, 2012. http://www.guardian.co.uk/commentisfree/libertycentral/2012/mar/13/turkey-enlightenment-journalists-prisons.

Gürsel, Seyfettin. "A Controversial Outlook of Turkish Economy." Paper presented at The U.S.-Turkey Commercial Relationship: A Growing Partnership, Hollings Center for International Dialogue, Istanbul, Turkey, 2012.

Hale, William. *Turkish Politics and the Military*. London: Routledge, 1994.

Healy, Geraldine, Mustafa Ozbilgin, and Hanife Aliefendioğlu. "Academic Employment and Gender: A Turkish Challenge to Vertical Sex Segregation." *European Journal of Industrial Relations* 11, no. 2 (2005): 247–64.

İdiz, Semih. "PM Erdoğan's Surprising Message in Cairo." *Hurriyet Daily News*, September 15, 2011. http://www.hurriyetdailynews.com/default.aspx?pageid=438&n=pm-erdogan8217s-surprising-message-in-cairo-2011-09-15.

İlkkaracan, İpek. "Why so Few Women in the Labor Market in Turkey?" *Feminist Economics* 18, no. 1 (2012): 1-37.

Jenkins, Gareth. "Continuity and Change: Prospects for Civil-Military Relations in Turkey." *International Affairs* 83, no. 2 (2007): 339–55.

Karpat, Kemal. "Historical Continuity and Identity Change." In *Ottoman Past and Today's Turkey*, ed. Kemal Karpat. Leiden, The Netherlands: Brill, 2000.

———. *Millets and Nationality: The Roots of Incongruity of Nation and State in the Post-Ottoman Era*, in *Christians and Jews in the Ottoman Empire*. New York: Holmes and Meier, 1982.

Kinzer, Stephen. "Ecevit, Ex-Skeptic, Leads Turkey's Switch on European Union." *New York Times*, December 21, 1999. http://www.nytimes.com/1999/12/21/world/ecevit-ex-skeptic-leads-turkey-s-switch-on-european-union.html.

Kitromilides, Paschalis M. "'Imagined Communities' and the National Origins of the National Question in the Balkans." *European History Quarterly* 19, no 2 (1989): 149–92.

Lehmann, Jean-Pierre. *"Turkey's 2023 Economic Goal in Global Perspective."* Istanbul: EDAM, 2011. http://edam.org.tr/eng/document/Lehmann-June%202011.pdf.

Letsch, Constanze. "Turkey Military Chiefs Resign over Sledgehammer 'Coup Plot' Arrests," Guardian, July 30, 2011. http://www.guardian.co.uk/world/2011/jul/30/turkey-military-chiefs-resign-sledgehammer.

Mardin, Şerif. "The Ottoman Empire." In *After Empire: Multiethnic Societies and Nation-Building: The Soviet Union and the Russian, Ottoman, and Habsburg Empires*, ed. Karen Barkey and Mark von Hagen. Boulder CO: Westview Press, 1997.

McCarthy, Justin. *The Arab World, Turkey and the Balkans (1878–1914): A Handbook of Historical Statistics*. Boston: G. K. Hall, 1982.

———. *Death and Exile: The Ethnic Cleansing of the Ottoman Muslims, 1821–1922*. Princeton NJ: Darwin Press, 1995.

Nasr, Vali. *Forces of Fortune: The Rise of the New Muslim Middle Class and What It Will Mean for Our World*. New York: Free Press, 2009.

Netherlands Scientific Council for Government Policy. *The European Union, Turkey and Islam*. Amsterdam: Amsterdam University Press, 2004.

Nişanyan, Sevan. *Hayali Coğrafyalar: Cumhuriyet Döneminde Türkiye'de Değiştirilen Yeradlar*. Istanbul: TESEV Yayınları, 2011.

Öcek, Tuğba. "Number of Libyan Tourists to Turkey Increases Sevenfold." *Today's Zaman*, August 3, 2012. http://www.todayszaman.com/newsDetail_getNewsById.action?newsId=288518.

Osborne, Lawrence. "Dreaming in Ottoman: Istanbul at a Crossroads." *Wall Street Journal*, August 23, 2012. http://online.wsj.com/article/SB10000872396390443855804577601322508049192.html.

Peker, Emre. "Turkey Gets Ratings Boost as S&P Plays Catch-Up." *Wall Street Journal*, March 28, 2013. http://blogs.wsj.com/emergingeurope/2013/03/28/turkey-gets-ratings-boost-as-sp-plays-catch-up/?mod=WSJBlog&mod=emergingeurope.

Pollock, David, and Soner Cagaptay. "What Happened to 'The Turkish Model'?" *Fikra Forum*, January 7, 2013, http://fikraforum.org/?p=2967.

Poulton, Hugh. *Who Are the Macedonians?* London: Hurst, 1995.

Rainsford, Sarah. "Two Faces of Modern Turkey." bbc, July 19, 2007. http://news.bbc.co.uk/2/hi/6906010.stm.

Reynolds, Michael. *Shattering Empires: The Clash and Collapse of the Ottoman and Russian Empires 1908-1918*. Cambridge: Cambridge University Press, 2011.

Tamimi, Jumana Al-. "Turkey Emerges as Tourism Hotspot for Gulf Visitors." Gulf-news.com, August 4, 2012. http://gulfnews.com/business/tourism/turkey-emerges-as-tourism-hotspot-for-gulf-visitors-1.1057513.

Telhami, Shibley. "Annual Arab Public Opinion Survey: 2011." Washington DC: Brookings Institution 2011.

Toprak, Binnaz. "*Political Power and Social Conservatism in Turkey*. Washington DC: Washington Institute for Near East Policy, 2009.

Turkey–2012 Progress Report: Enlargement Strategy and Main Challenges. Brussels, Belgium: European Commission, 2012.

Turkish Automative Industry Report. Ankara: Republic of Turkey Prime Ministry and Deloitte, 2010.

"Turkish Politics: The Ephemeral Alevi Opening." *Economist*, August 11, 2012.

Turkish Statistical Institute. "Income and Living Conditions Survey, 2011." September 17, 2012. http://www.turkstat.gov.tr/PreHaberBultenleri.do?id=10902.

United States. Bureau of Democracy, Human Rights, and Labor. *Turkey: International Religious Freedom Report* 2006. Washington DC: U.S. Department of State, 2006. http://www.state.gov/j/ drl/rls/irf/2006/71413.htm.

Vicky, Alain. "Turkey Moves into Africa." *Le Monde*, May 2011. http://mondediplo.com/2011/05/08turkey.

Weiss, Michael. "Syrian Rebels Say Turkey Is Arming and Training Them." *Telegraph* (London), May 22, 2012. http://blogs.telegraph.co.uk/news/michaelweiss/100159613/syrian-rebels-say-turkey-is-arming-and-training-them/.

"Women's Economic Opportunity Index 2012," accessed at the *Economist*, https://www.eiu.com/public/topical_report.aspx?campaignid=weoindex2012.

Yıldız, Ahmet. *Ne Mutlu Türküm Diyebilene: Türk Ulusal Kimliğinin Etno-Seküler Sınırları (1919–1938)*. Istanbul: İletişim Yayınları, 2001.

Zarakol, Ayse. *After Defeat: How the East Learned to Live with the West*. Cambridge: Cambridge University Press, 2011.

Zeydanlıoğlu, Welat. "Turkey's Kurdish Language Policy." *International Journal of the Sociology of Language* 2012, no. 217 (2012): 99–125.

Index